VANESSA CHRISTENSON of V and CO.

make it sew modern

Gather, Twist, Pleat, Texture

CREDITS

President & CEO: Tom Wierzbicki

Editor in Chief: Mary V. Green

Design Director: Paula Schlosser

Managing Editor: Karen Costello Soltys

Technical Editor: Christine Barnes

Copy Editor: Sheila Chapman Ryan

Production Manager: Regina Girard

Cover & Text Designer: Adrienne Smitke

Illustrator: Laurel Strand

Photographer: Brent Kane

Make It Sew Modern: Gather, Twist, Pleat, Texture
© 2012 by Vanessa Christenson

That Patchwork Place® is an imprint of Martingale & Company®.

Martingale & Company
19021 120th Ave. NE, Ste. 102
Bothell, WA 98011-9511 USA
www.martingale-pub.com

Printed in China
17 16 15 14 13 12   8 7 6 5 4 3 2 1

Library of Congress Cataloging-in-Publication Data is available upon request.

ISBN: 978-1-60468-059-1

Contents

INTRODUCTION

Making things prettier is a passion with me, and the reason I decided to write this book. You can always make a plain pillow or a handbag, but what if you add a ruffle here, a gather there? Won't it be that much more appealing and that much more loved? In my home I like clean lines, but I also want texture and some softer lines. Adding texture by manipulating fabric is an exciting, fun way to create beautiful things that you'll love to have around you—or love to give away to special people in your life.

In this book you'll find a collection of projects based on creative techniques with fabric. The first section focuses on adding ruffles to adorn all sorts of projects. You'll notice that I have a special place in my heart for pillows and flowers. One of my favorite projects is the Throw Pillow with Frosting (page 9), and it was while I was working on this pillow that I felt a spark of inspiration that kept me going with other ruffled designs. The second and third sections show you how to twist and gather fabric to make a bracelet, a cascading scarf, a quilt with softly gathered borders, and much more. In the final section you'll see how I use pleats to enhance some of my favorite things, like a handy tote, a modern pillow, and a skirt I made for my daughter.

I myself am a mother of four, so I understand being short on time and cash. Accordingly, most of the projects in this book are quick and easy, and always with a budget in mind. I really hope that when you pick up this book, you'll be inspired to make something (while your kids nap or are in school) that will make you happy—and won't break the bank. It makes *me* happy to create them for you. So, let's get started!

Ruffles

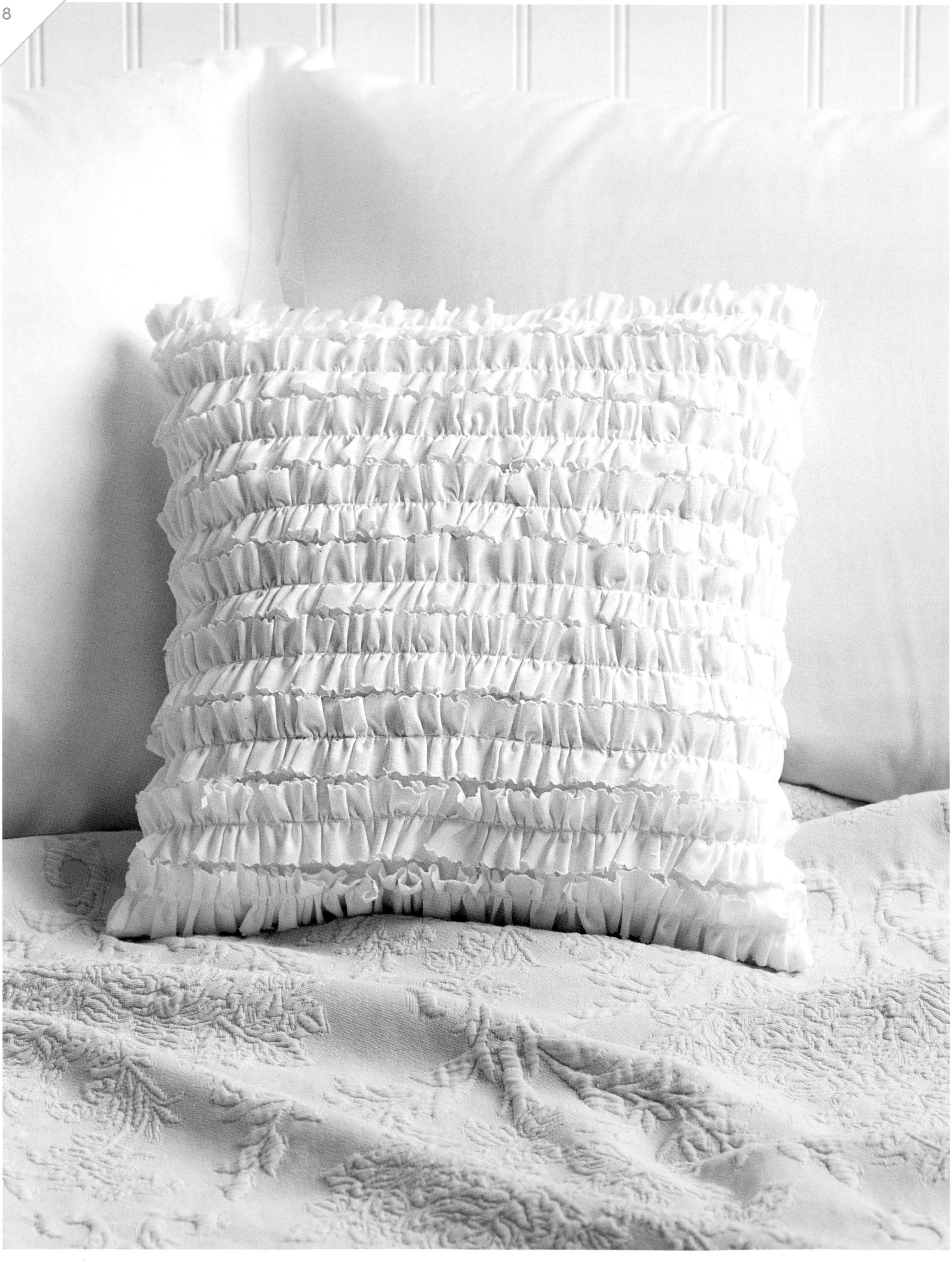

THROW PILLOW with Frosting

Finished size: 14" x 14"

One of the first pillows I made for my daughter's "big-girl" bed, and still one of my favorites, this ruffled pillow will make any young lady's bed that much more girly.

Materials

Yardage is based on 42"-wide fabric.

1 yard of cotton fabric
Pinking rotary cutter, mat, and ruler (or pinking shears)
Water-soluble marker
Cluster Stuff or fiberfill, 16-ounce bag

Cutting

From the cotton fabric, cut:
2 squares, 14½" x 14½"
9 strips, 1½" x 42", cut with pinking rotary cutter or pinking shears*

*To cut these strips using a pinking rotary cutter, trim the fabric edge with the cutter; then measure 1½" from the trimmed edge and begin cutting strips. To cut with pinking shears, measure 1½"-wide strips and mark with a water-soluble marker; cut on the marked lines.

Assembling the Pillow

Use ¼" seam allowances.

1. Set your sewing machine on the longest (basting) stitch. Sew down the middle of each strip to gather the fabric, holding the top thread with your index finger and thumb, near the spool, to increase the tension on the thread; see "Machine Ruffles and Gathers" (page 91).
2. Working on the right side of one of the fabric squares, pin a ruffle ½" from the left edge. The ends of the ruffles will overlap the upper and lower edges of the square; don't trim them yet. ❶

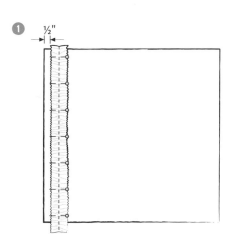

3. Pin the remaining ruffles so their edges just touch. Set your sewing machine to the regular stitch and sew each ruffle on top of the gathering stitches through both layers. Trim the ruffle tails. ❷

4. With right sides together, pin the plain square and the ruffled square. Sew around the perimeter, leaving a 4" opening for turning along one edge parallel to the strips. ❸

5. Turn the pillow right side out and stuff. Hand stitch the opening closed using a ladder stitch (page 91).

❷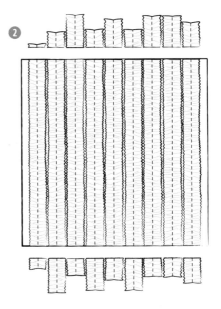

❸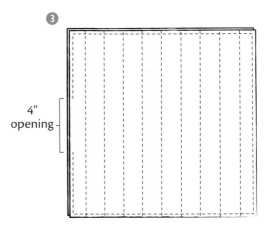

4"
opening

Cascading Spring SCARF

Finished size: Approximately 8" x 60"

This scarf is a stylish addition to any wardrobe. I especially love the way the ruffles fall—it reminds me of a cascading waterfall. To create the ruffles, you'll use elastic thread in the bobbin and regular thread to match the fabric on the top.

Materials

½ yard of 60"-wide jersey (lightweight knit) fabric
⅛ yard of 42"-wide matching or coordinating cotton fabric
Water-soluble marker
Elastic thread
Bias tape maker

Cutting

From the jersey fabric, cut:
2 strips, 8" x 60"

From the cotton fabric, cut:
2 strips, 1" x 42"

Assembling the Scarf

Use ¼" seam allowances unless otherwise indicated.

1. Pin the two jersey 8" x 60" strips right sides together and end to end; stitch along the short edges. Press the seam allowances open.
2. Working on the wrong side, mark the center of the strip along the full length using the water-soluble marker. ❶
3. Wind the elastic thread onto a bobbin by hand or by machine. You'll need to wind the elastic on the tighter side, which is easy enough to do by hand. To wind it by machine, hold the top thread with your thumb and index finger, near the spool, to increase the tension.

❶
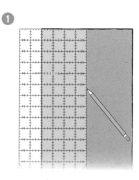

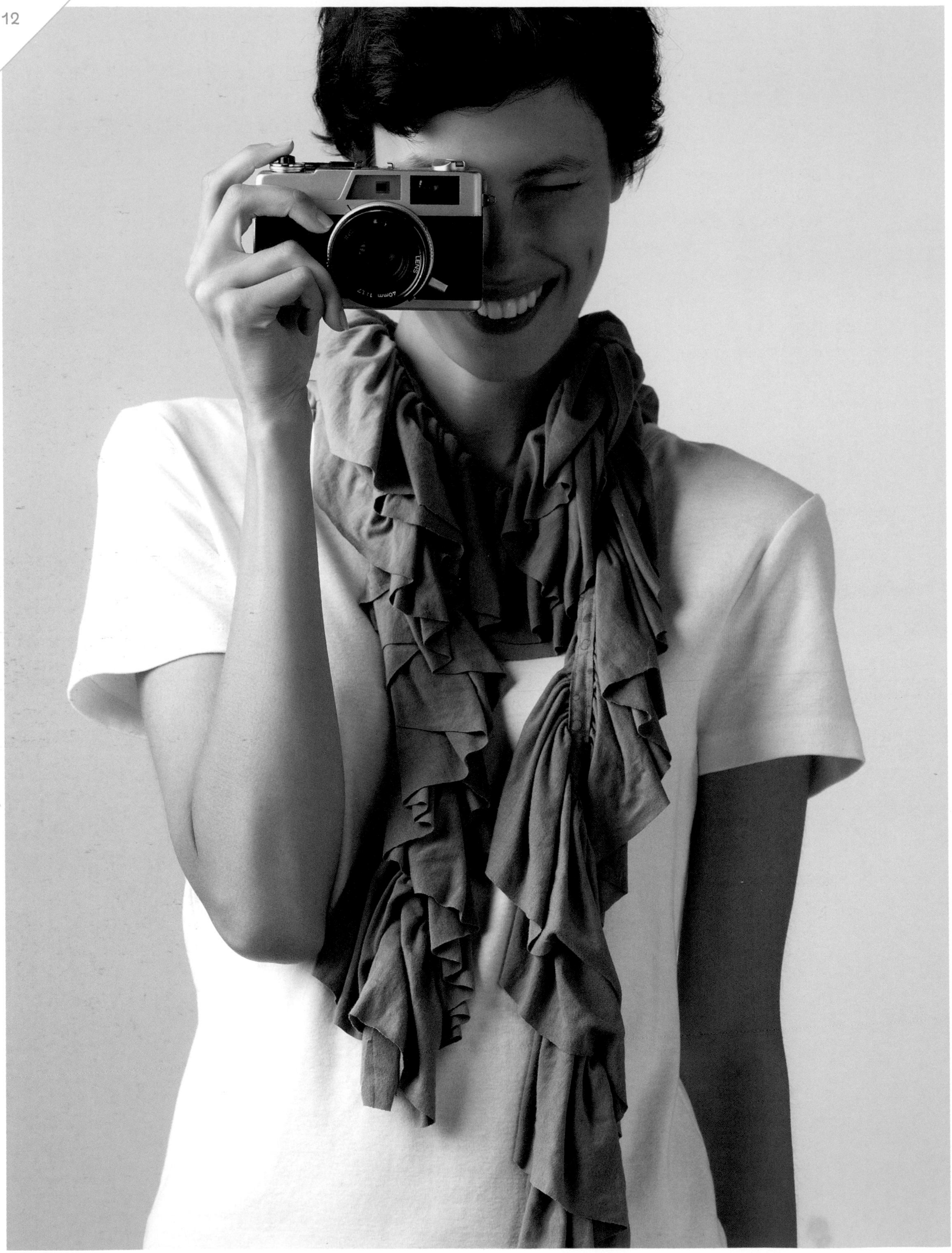

4. Set your sewing machine on the longest (basting) stitch. With the wrong side of the fabric facing up, sew ⅛" to ¼" on both sides of the marked line to gather the fabric; see "Machine Ruffles and Gathers" (page 91). ❷

5. Switch to regular thread in the bobbin. Sew the two cotton strips together end to end to make one long strip; press the seam allowances open. Use the bias tape maker to create tape, following the manufacturer's directions. Press the tape flat. ❸

6. Lay the tape on the right side of the ruffled jersey strip to cover the elastic thread. Pin; stitch close to the fold on each edge. ❹

7. Cut off the excess tape at each end, leaving a 1" tail. Fold each tail to the wrong side, turning under the raw edge, and press. Stitch by hand to secure. ❺

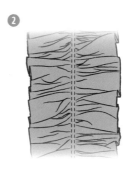

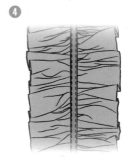

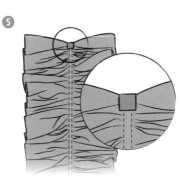

CASCADING SPRING SCARF

Decorative Hanging GLOBES

Finished size: 5" and 7" balls

I created these balls with a wedding in mind, but you can use them to decorate a little girl's room or, when made in summery colors, to create a lovely environment for an outdoor party.

Materials

Yardage is based on 60"-wide fabric.

1⅜ yards of jersey (lightweight knit) fabric for each 6" Styrofoam ball

⅞ yard of jersey for each 4" Styrofoam ball

4" and 6" Styrofoam balls*

Hot-glue gun and glue sticks

Krazy glue

Approximately 1¼ yards of ⅞"-wide coordinating ribbon for each ball

*4" Styrofoam balls typically come in packs of six; 6" balls, in packs of two.

Cutting

1. Fold the fabric in half lengthwise to make cutting easier. Trim the selvages.
2. For each 6" ball, cut the fabric across the width into 46 strips, 1" x 60". For each 4" ball, cut the fabric into 30 strips, 1" x 60".
3. For both sizes, cut each strip in half to create two 30" strips.

Assembling the Balls

Use ¼" seam allowances.

1. Set your sewing machine to the longest (basting) stitch. To gather each strip along one edge, see "Machine Ruffles and Gathers" (page 91). Each ruffled strip will curl over on itself. ❶

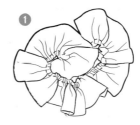

2. Roll a ruffled strip along the stitched edge, creating a flower; trim the thread ends. Dab hot glue onto the end of the strip to secure the flower. Repeat with the remaining strips. ❷

Dab glue.

3. Apply hot glue all over the back of one flower and adhere it to the Styrofoam ball. ❸

Glue

4. Continue to glue and attach the flowers to the ball, placing them closely so their tops touch and there are no gaps. Continue until you've covered half the ball.

5. Cut a piece of ribbon to the desired length. Dab Krazy Glue onto the ribbon end and attach it to the ball using three or four pins. Let dry; then apply more glue to the top of the ribbon. ❹

6. Once the glue has dried and the ribbon is secure, continue attaching flowers to cover the ball.

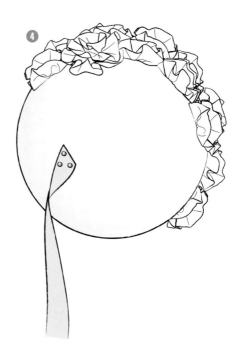

Spring-Blossom WREATH

Finished size: 13"-wide wreath

This project takes a bit of time and hot glue, but the outcome is fantastic. Hang it from your front door to welcome guests, or in front of a mirror or armoire to increase the wow factor in any room.

Materials

Yardage is based on 58"–66"-wide fabric.

2¼ yards of gold jersey (lightweight knit) fabric

12" Styrofoam wreath

Hot-glue gun and glue sticks

Optional: 3" x 18" strip of cotton or jersey fabric for hanging

Cutting

1. Fold the fabric in half lengthwise to make cutting easier. Trim the selvages.
2. Cut the fabric across the width to make 66 strips, each 1" wide. Cut each strip in half to make 132 strips.

Making the Flowers

Use ¼" seam allowances.

1. Set your sewing machine to the longest (basting) stitch. To gather each strip along one edge, see "Machine Ruffles and Gathers" (page 91). Each ruffled strip will curl over on itself. ❶
2. Roll a ruffled strip along the stitched edge to make a flower; trim the thread ends. Dab hot glue onto the end of the strip to secure the flower. Repeat with the remaining strips. ❷

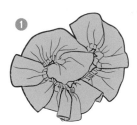

Dab glue.

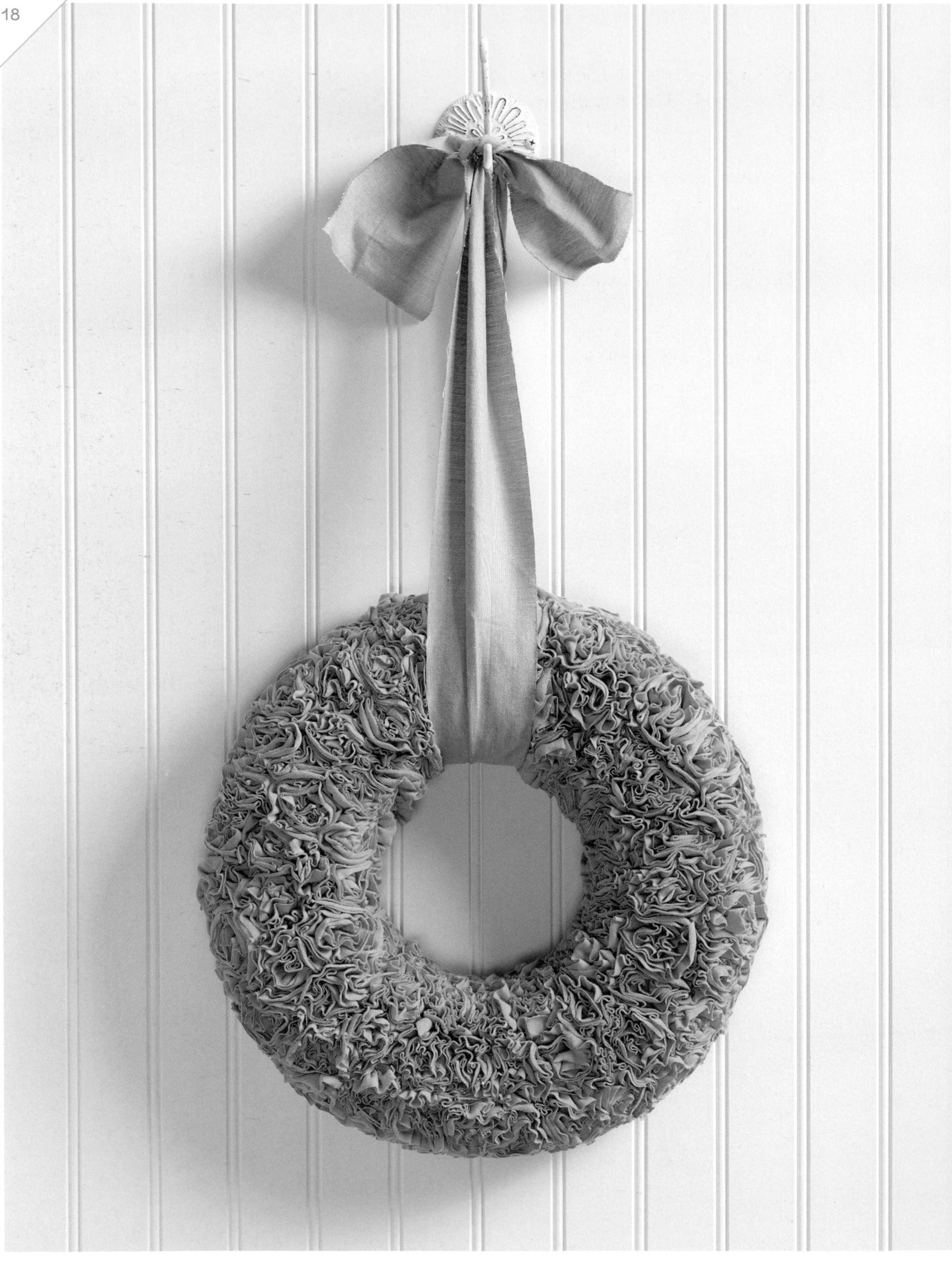

3. Apply hot glue all over the back of one flower and adhere it to the wreath along the back edge where the curved surface meets the flat back. ❸

4. Attach another flower next to the first one so their edges touch. ❹

5. Attach a third flower slightly in front of the first two to fill in the gap. ❺

6. Continue to fill in with flowers, making sure none of the white wreath shows. ❻

7. Optional: loop the 3" x 18" strip of fabric through the wreath and tie in a knot for hanging.

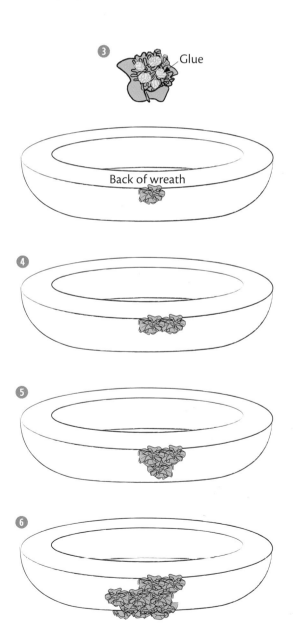

SPRING-BLOSSOM WREATH

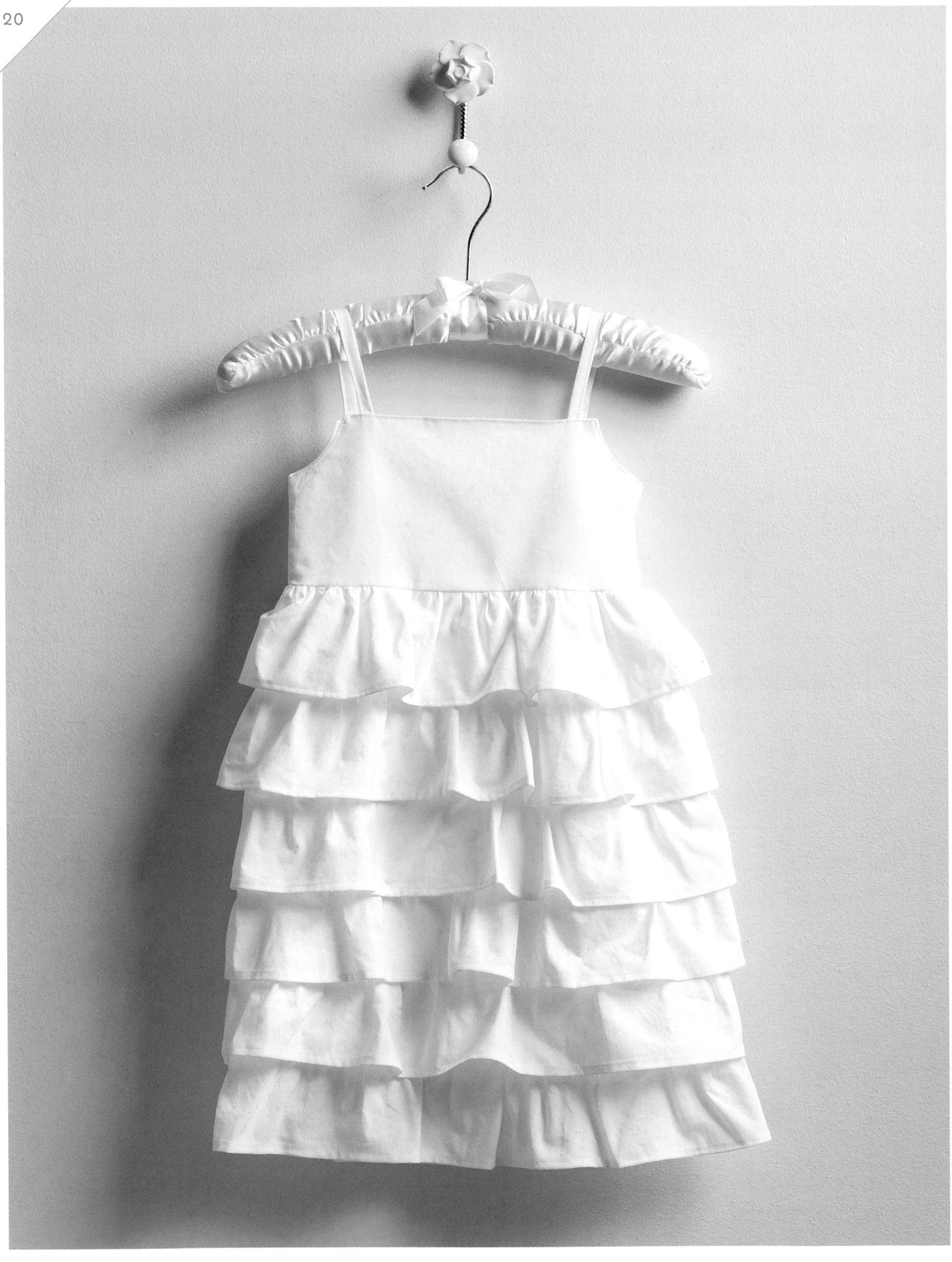

Picture-Perfect DRESS

Finished size: 4T (fits 4- to 5-year-old girl, but can be customized)

This dress is for the little girl in your life who loves to feel pretty and frilly. Perfect for the summer months or dressed up with a cardigan in cooler weather, it's sure to be one of her favorites.

Materials

Yardage is based on 42"-wide fabric.

2¾ yards of white cotton fabric for dress*
2" of ⅛"-wide elastic for button loop
CD for armhole template
Water-soluble marker
Small button

*The model shown is size 4T. See "Measuring for a Custom Fit" (below) to calculate the yardage for other sizes.

Cutting

From the white fabric, cut:
2 pieces equal to bodice front width x bodice length
2 pieces equal to bodice back width x bodice length
1 piece equal to skirt width x skirt length
2 strips, 1½" x 12"
5 strips, 4½" x skirt width + 10"*

*You may need to cut more ruffle strips for a larger-sized dress.

Measuring for a Custom Fit

Take the following measurements to ensure that the finished dress fits your child:

- **Bodice width.** Measure around the chest. Divide this measurement by two and add 1" for the *bodice front width* and 1½" for the *bodice back width*.
- **Bodice length.** Measure from 2" above the armpit (where it forms the crease) to where you want the bodice to end; add ½" for two seam allowances to achieve the *bodice length*. For an empire waist, the lower edge of the bodice is 2" below the armpit, for a total bodice length of 4½".
- **Skirt width.** Measure around the widest part of the child's hips. Add 10" for the *skirt width*.
- **Skirt length.** Measure from the point where you want the bodice to end to where you want the skirt to end, such as from the waist to the knee. Add 1" for the *skirt length*.

Based on these measurements, add up the bodice length and the skirt length, plus 22½" for five ruffles (for each extra ruffle, add 4½"). Add 10% to this total, divide by 36, and round up to the nearest ¼ yard to arrive at the yardage needed.

Making the Bodice Back and Front

Use ¼" seam allowances unless otherwise indicated.

1. Cut the bodice back rectangles in half vertically in preparation for the center back seam. With right sides together, pin one set of bodice back pieces along the edges you just cut. Fold the elastic piece in half to make a loop and insert it between the fabric layers, ½" from the top edges with the loop facing inward and the ends extending outward; pin. Stitch, catching the ends of the elastic in the seam and stopping at the midpoint as shown. ❶

2. Repeat with the remaining bodice back pieces (without the elastic), stopping at the same place. Press the seam allowances open just to the point where you stopped stitching.

3. With right sides together, pin the bodice sets along the raw edges. Stitch each seam separately, backstitching at the midpoints. Press the seam allowances open. ❷

4. Turn the bodice back right side out and press the sewn edges for a crisp finish. You now have a lined bodice back with a neckline opening and a button loop. ❸

5. With the bodice front rectangles right sides together, use the CD to mark the armhole curves as shown. Trim on the marked lines. ❹

6. Unfold the rectangles to make two layers. With right sides still together, stitch along the curves to create the armhole edges. ❺

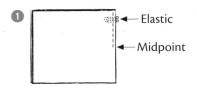

❶ ← Elastic
← Midpoint

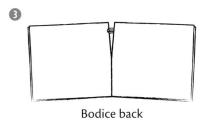

❷

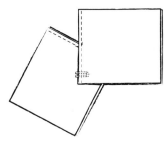

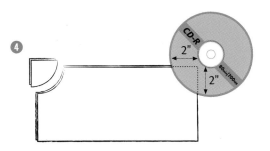

❸

Bodice back

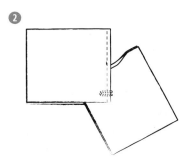

❹ 2"
2"

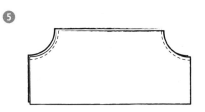

❺

7. Turn the bodice back pieces inside out and mark, trim, and sew the arm-hole curves.

8. Hand sew the button on the bodice back, ½" from the top edge and opposite the loop.

Attaching the Straps

1. Fold, press, and topstitch the 1½" strips; see "Straps" (page 93).

2. Measure from 2" above your child's armpit on the front, over the shoulder, to 2" above the armpit on the back. Add 1" to this measurement. Trim the straps to this length.

3. Sandwich the straps between the layers of the bodice front so the strap ends are ¼" above the top edge of the bodice and are approximately ½" from the armhole seams. Pin the layers, including the straps. ❻

4. Stitch the top edge of the bodice, backstitching over the straps for strength. Turn the bodice right side out and press.

5. Lay the bodice back, wrong side out, on your work surface with the bodice front as shown. Slip the ends of the straps between the bodice back layers, aligning the straps as you did on the front. Pin and stitch the layers; turn right side out and press. ❼

Tip: If you're using a printed fabric for the dress and a plain fabric for the bodice lining, make sure the *lining* fabric is face down on both the bodice front and bodice back, even though the bodice front is right side out and the bodice back is wrong side out.

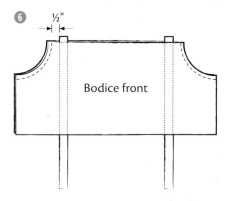

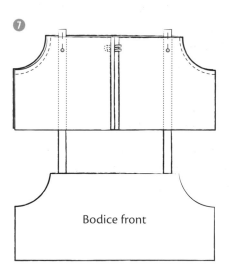

Completing the Bodice

1. Open the bodice front and the bodice back on one side and pin the pieces right sides together, matching the seams; stitch. Press the seam allowances open. Repeat for the opposite side seam. **8**

2. Press the finished bodice and topstitch (page 93) the armhole curves, back opening edges, and top edges.

Making the Skirt

1. With right sides together, sew the skirt along the short edges, making a tube. Press the seam allowances open. Fold the skirt into fourths at the upper edge in preparation for adding the ruffles and mark each spot with a pin or water-soluble marker.

> **Tip:** If your fabric has a directional pattern (page 90), decide now which will be the top edge of the skirt.

2. Fold ¼" to the wrong side of the skirt on the bottom edge; press. Repeat to make a double-fold hem; stitch. Turn the skirt right side out.

Attaching the Ruffles

1. With right sides together, sew a 4½" ruffle strip along the short ends to create a loop. Press the seam allowances open.

2. Fold and stitch a double-fold hem along the lower raw edge of the ruffle loop. Turn the loop right side out.

3. Set your sewing machine on the longest (basting) stitch. Baste the unhemmed edge of the loop, starting at the seam and ending at the other side of the seam. Do not overlap the stitching.

4. To distribute the ruffle evenly around the skirt, fold the loop into quarters as you did the upper edge of the skirt and mark with pins or a water-soluble marker.

5. With *right sides facing up*, pin the ruffle to the top edge of the skirt, aligning the ruffle seam and the skirt seam. Pin the ruffle on the opposite side of the skirt, matching the pins or marks. Pin the ruffle at the center front and center back of the skirt, again matching the pins or marks. **9**

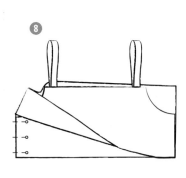

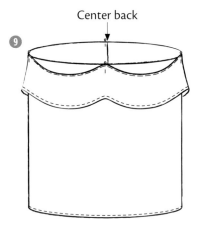

Center back

6. Gently pull the basting thread on the ruffle to gather it, distributing the fullness as you go. Once the ruffle is gathered to fit the skirt, pin all around. **10**

7. Using a scant ¼" seam allowance and a narrow zigzag stitch, sew the ruffle onto the skirt. (A narrower seam allowance and zigzag stitch ensure that the zigzagging will be covered when you sew the skirt to the bodice.)

8. Fold this ruffle up and away from the skirt. Measure 2½" from the seam of the first ruffle and mark the skirt with a water-soluble marker. **11**

9. Repeat the process to make additional ruffles and stitch them to the skirt until you run out of space. I sewed a ruffle at the edge of the hem to make my skirt a little longer.

Tip: To distribute the ruffles evenly around the skirt as you work your way down, fold the lower skirt and the ruffles into quarters and mark.

Attaching the Skirt to the Bodice

1. Using a basting stitch and starting at the side seam, baste ⅛" around the top of the skirt, leaving 5" of thread at the beginning and end.

2. With right sides together and raw edges aligned, pin the bodice to the skirt, matching a bodice side seam to the skirt seam. Gently pull one of the basting threads to gather the skirt to the bodice, distributing the fullness as you go. Pin the bodice to the skirt.

3. Reset your machine to its regular stitch length and sew the bodice to the skirt, stitching just below the zigzagging on the first ruffle.

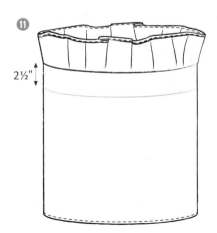

2½"

Twisting

Flower-Bouquet PILLOW

Finished size: 13½" x 13½"

Strips that twist and turn transform a simple pillow into a stylish accent. Add some color or go neutral—either way, the texture is sure to attract attention.

Materials

Yardage is based on 42"-wide fabric.

½ yard or 2 fat quarters of beige cotton or linen fabric for pillow

⅛ yard each of three different solid-color fabrics for flowers*

Cluster Stuff or fiberfill, 16-ounce bag

You need only two 2" strips of each color, so you can use scraps to total approximately 80" each.

Cutting

From the beige fabric, cut:
2 squares, 14" x 14"

From *each* of the solid colors, cut:
2 strips, 2" x 42"

Making the Flowers

Use ¼" seam allowances.

1. Fold the end of one strip lengthwise, wrong sides together, to make a strip 1" wide. Fold again to make the end ½" wide. ❶

2. Start the first flower at one corner of a beige square, at least 3" from the edges. Stitch across the end of the strip to secure it. ❷

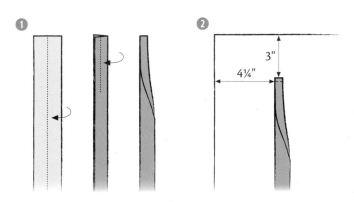

3. Gently twist the strip outward. ❸

4. Sew the twisted strip to the pillow fabric, curving it as you go and sewing ¼" from the inside edge so the stitching will be covered by the next "round." ❹

5. Continue to twist and sew the strip to make a complete circle; then work inward, overlapping the edges to prevent gaps. If the strip runs out before you complete the flower, start another strip, backstitching to secure the end. ❺

6. Once you fill in the shape, backstitch and trim the strip close to the backstitching. ❻

7. Attach two more flowers in the same way, overlapping them slightly to create the look of a bouquet.

Assembling the Pillow

1. With right sides together, pin and stitch the pillow pieces around the perimeter, leaving a 4" opening along the bottom edge for turning. To avoid pointy corners on your pillow, see "Pillow Corners" (page 92). ❼

2. Turn the pillow right side out, stuff, and hand stitch the opening closed using a ladder stitch (page 91).

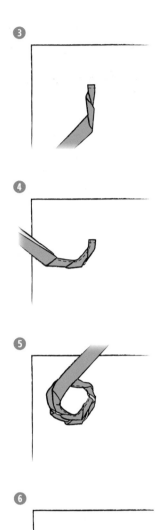

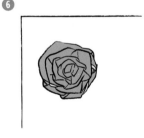

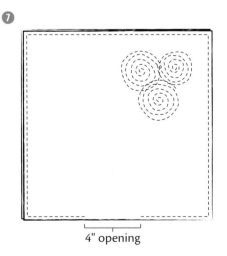

4" opening

Flower RING

Finished size: Approximately 1" wide

Dress up an outfit or add a little color to your day with this "fabric bling." Whatever look you're trying to accomplish, this little ring is sure to become a must-have accessory!

Materials

1 fabric strip, 1" x 10"
Adjustable ring blank
Hot-glue gun and glue sticks
Krazy Glue

Making the Flower Ring

1. Dab a bit of hot glue on the wrong side of the strip at one end. Fold the strip in half lengthwise, wrong sides together. Glue and fold the strip again to make the end ¼" wide. ❶

2. Apply a bit more glue to the end and fold the strip forward to adhere it. This end serves as the base of the flower. ❷

3. Twist the strip inward, not too tight but not too loose. Dab glue onto the base and secure the twisted strip to it. ❸

4. Continue to twist the strip, applying glue to secure each new twist to the previous one and nestling each round slightly under the previous round. ❹

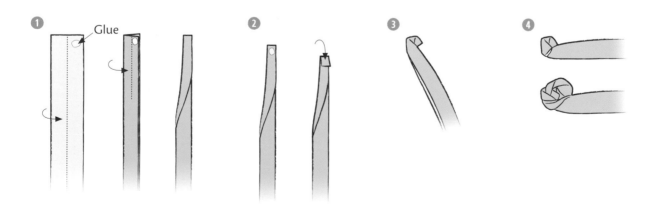

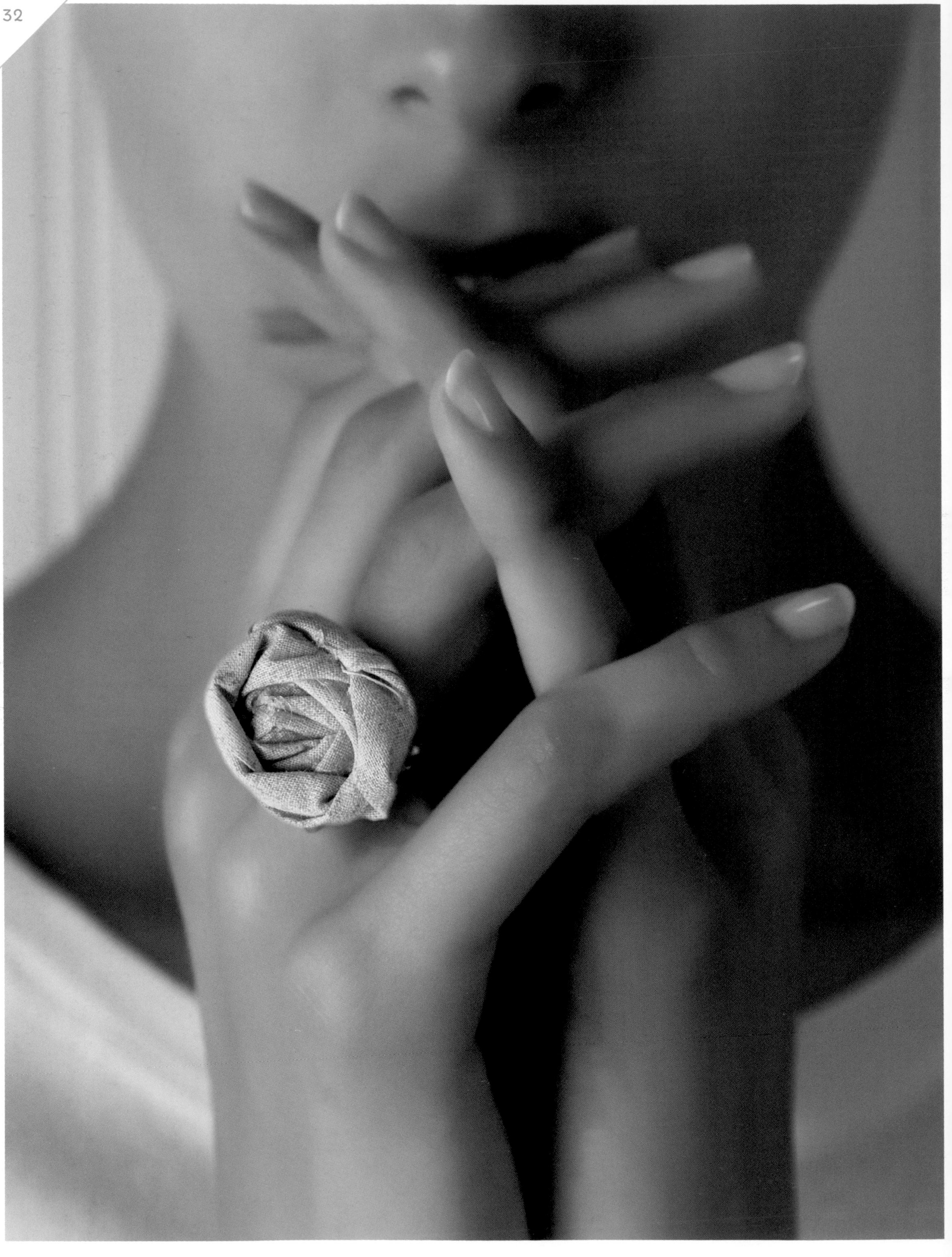

5. Make the flower as large as you like, leaving a fabric tail. **⑤**
6. Tuck the edge under and glue it to the base. Trim the excess tail. **⑥**
7. Apply Krazy Glue to the base of the flower and adhere it to the ring blank, pressing firmly until the glue is set.

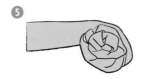

Satin-Ribbon FLOWER ACCESSORY

Finished size: Approximately 5" diameter

Decorate an outfit or a purse with this ribbon flower, or attach it to a hair clip for the perfect accessory. Of all the flowers I've created, this is by far my favorite.

Materials

1⅝ yards of 1½"-wide pink satin ribbon for petals and center

Felt circle, approximately 2" in diameter

Fray Check

Hot-glue gun and glue sticks

Krazy Glue

Pin back or alligator hair clip

Cutting

From the pink ribbon, cut:

6 pieces, 2½" long

6 pieces, 2" long

1 piece, 10" long

Assembling the Flower

1. Apply Fray Check to the cut edges of each ribbon piece to prevent raveling; let dry.
2. Working on the wrong (dull) side of a 2½" ribbon piece, dab a bit of hot glue onto the raw end about a third of the way from the left edge. Fold the top-left corner onto the glue; repeat for the top-right corner. Glue and fold the top edge. Repeat for the remaining ribbon pieces to make 12 petals. ❶

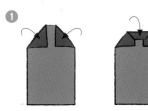

3. Dab hot glue onto the wrong side of a 2½" petal at the midpoint of the bottom edge. Attach the petal to cover half of the felt circle. ❷

4. At the base of the petal, make a pleat on either side, bringing the folds inward to meet at the center. Dab glue between the layers to adhere the pleats. ❸

5. Attach and pleat the second petal directly opposite the first one so the petals touch at the center of the circle. ❹

6. Attach the third and fourth petals so they slightly overlap the first two. ❺

7. Turn the flower around and attach the remaining petals to complete the bottom layer of the flower.

8. Dab glue onto the center of the flower. Attach and pleat a 2" petal to cover the gap between two bottom petals, with the raw edge of this new petal in the center of the circle. ❻

9. Continue to attach 2" petals to complete the top layer. ❼

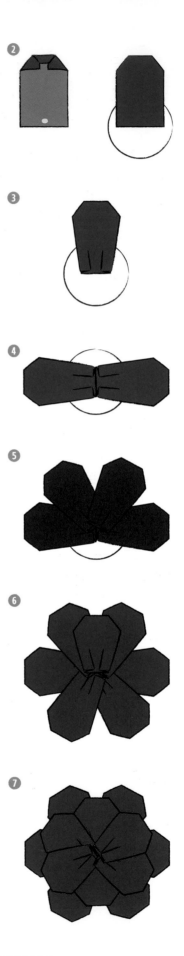

Making the Flower Center

1. Dab Fray Check onto the end of the 10" piece of ribbon for the flower center; let it dry.

2. To create the flower-center base, see steps 1 and 2 of "Making the Flower Ring" (page 31). When folded, the end of the ribbon will be ⅜" wide.

3. Twist the ribbon inward, not too tight but not too loose. Dab glue onto the base and secure the twirled ribbon to it. ❽

4. Continue to twist the ribbon, applying a dab of glue to secure each new twist to the previous one. ❾

5. Make the flower center large enough to cover the glue at the base of the petals. Leave a ribbon tail. To complete the flower center, see step 6 of "Making the Flower Ring" (page 33).

6. Apply glue to the bottom of the flower center and adhere it to the petals.

7. Turn the flower over so the felt circle is facing up. To make a pin, apply Krazy Glue approximately ¼" from the edge of the felt circle and adhere it to the pin back, pressing firmly until the glue is set. For a hair accessory, apply glue to the middle of the felt circle. Place the top half of the alligator clip in the glue, making sure the bottom half doesn't touch the glue until it is set.

Decorative BALLS

Finished size: Approximately 4"

Making a house a home means paying attention to the details. What better way to create the look you want than with these decorative fabric balls?

Materials

Yardage is based on 42"-wide fabric.

¼ yard of cotton fabric for each ball
4" Styrofoam ball*
Hot-glue gun and glue sticks

*These typically come in a pack of six.

Cutting

From the cotton fabric, cut:
4 strips, 1" x 42", for each ball

Making the Balls

1. To fold the first strip, see step 1 of "Making the Flower Ring" (page 31).
2. Apply glue to the Styrofoam ball and attach the folded end of the strip to the ball. ❶
3. Twist the strip for a few inches. Dab a bit of glue onto the end of the folded strip where it attaches to the ball. Coil the twisted strip and glue it to the ball to cover the end. ❷

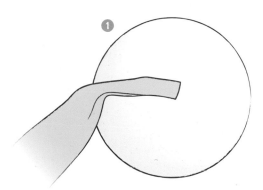

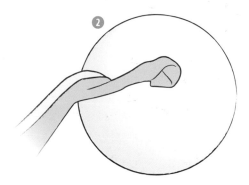

4. Continue to twist the strip and adhere it to the ball, applying glue to both the ball and the base of the coil so the twisted strip lies flat. **3**

5. When you run out of the first strip, flatten the end slightly to the side and glue it to the ball. Repeat step 1 to attach a new strip, overlapping the end of the first strip and twisting the new strip immediately. **4**

6. Once the ball is covered, trim the end and squish it into the center of the coil. **5**

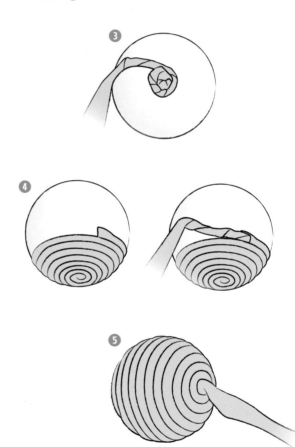

Twisted-Fabric BRACELET

Finished size: Approximately 3" in diameter

This is one of the most popular patterns I've designed. You'll be able to create these simple bracelets for yourself and all your friends in an afternoon.

Materials (for two bracelets)

Yardage is based on 42"-wide fabric.

⅜ yard of cotton fabric
One pack (2 yards) of Wright's ⁶⁄₃₂" Cotton Filler
    Cord or other similar cording
Hot-glue gun and glue sticks (optional)
1¾"- or 1⅞"-long pins
Long needle and thimble
Thread to blend

Cutting

From the cotton fabric, cut:
3 strips, 1½" x 42", for each bracelet

From the cotton filler cord, cut:
1 piece, 31" long, for each bracelet

Making the Bracelet

1. Sew the three strips together end to end to make one long strip. Press the seam allowances open. Fold one end of the strip in half lengthwise, wrong sides together.
2. Machine stitch the folded end of the strip to one end of the cording to anchor the strip. You can also glue the strip end to the cording. ❶
3. Tightly twist and wrap the folded fabric strip around the cording. ❷

> **Tip:** If you have trouble keeping the fabric in place, apply a dab of hot glue to the cording every few inches.

❶

❷

4. Continue to twist the fabric strip as you wind it around the cording, overlapping it here and there to make it look chunkier. In some places I let the wrong side of the fabric show for a less-polished look.

5. When you reach the end of the cording, sew or glue the end of the strip to the cording.

6. To make sure you'll be able to slip the bracelet on and off your wrist, loop the covered cording around your wrist and pin to mark the first loop. Remove. ❸

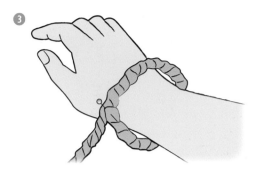

7. Loop the rest of the covered cording for a total of three times, until it's opposite the point where you started. Stick long pins through the three loops to secure them. You may have some covered cording left over, depending on the size of your loops. ❹

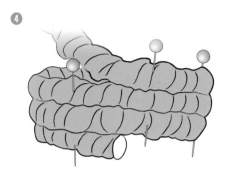

8. Stitch back and forth across the fabric and cording at the end of the last coil to "seal" it. Cut the excess cording.

9. Tuck the ends of the cording to the inside of the bracelet and hand stitch in place. ❺

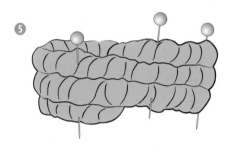

10. Here's where your thimble comes into play. Using two strands of thread and a long needle, come up through one of the outer coils where the coil starts and stops, hiding the knot. Sew through the bracelet from top to bottom, pushing the needle through all three coils with the thimble and pulling the thread through. Insert the needle back into the bracelet about ½" from the first stitch and again sew through the coils. Continue stitching until you've worked your way around the bracelet. Take a few tiny, tight stitches at the end and clip close to the bracelet. ❻

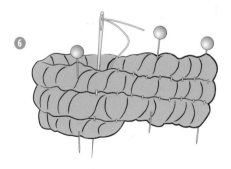

Gathering

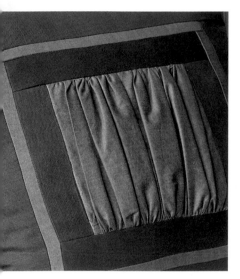

Appliqué Doily QUILT

Finished size: 43" x 50½"

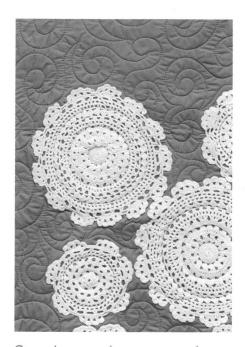

Simple yet elegant, with its gathered borders and doily appliqués, this quilt has wonderful texture for the eye to see and for your baby to feel.

Materials

Yardage is based on 42"-wide fabric.

2¾ yards of gray solid for quilt center, outer borders, and binding*

1¼ yards of white cotton fabric for gathered inner borders

2⅞ yards of fabric for backing

51" x 58½" piece of batting

7 doilies in assorted sizes for appliqués**

Temporary spray adhesive

Hand-sewing needle

Yardage is for strips cut lengthwise, eliminating seams in the outer borders. If you prefer to cut cross-wise strips and piece the borders (and binding), you'll need 2¼ yards.

**The doilies shown here measure 5" and 9" in diameter.*

Cutting

From the lengthwise grain of the gray solid, cut:
1 rectangle, 36" x 43½"
4 strips, 3" x length of fabric
5 strips, 2½" x length of fabric

From the lengthwise grain of the white fabric, cut:
10 strips, 2½" x length of fabric

Appliquéing the Doilies

Use ¼" seam allowances unless otherwise indicated.

1. Arrange the doilies in the lower-right corner of the gray rectangle, allowing 1" to 3" between the doilies and the raw edges.
2. Working one at a time, spray temporary adhesive on the back of each doily and adhere it to the fabric.

3. Attach the doilies to the fabric using a running stitch or appliqué stitch (page 89).

Making the Gathered Borders

1. Trim two white strips to 39" and two strips to 43½". Set these strips aside; they will become the foundation for the gathered strips.

2. From the remaining six white strips, cut two in half crosswise to make four half-length strips. Sew a half strip to each full-length strip, end to end, to make four long strips for gathering. Press the seam allowances open.

3. To gather the white strips, set the sewing machine on the longest (basting) stitch and pull at least 5" of thread to release some gathers later, if necessary. Hold the top thread between your thumb and forefinger, near the spool, to put tension on the thread; see "Machine Ruffles and Gathers" (page 91). Stitch the length of the first strip. At the end, pull at least 5" of thread.

4. Gather the opposite long edge in the same manner. Repeat to gather the remaining long strips. ❶

5. With right sides facing up, layer a gathered strip on a 43½" white strip, distributing the gathers so the top strip is the same length as the strip underneath. Pin. ❷

6. Stitch each long edge of the layered strips using a basting stitch. Repeat with the remaining 43½" white strip and a gathered strip to make the opposite side border.

7. Prepare the remaining gathered strips and the two 39" strips for the top and bottom borders. Before you layer and stitch these strips, compare them to the side border strips and, if necessary, release a bit of the gathers so the fullness is similar.

Attaching the Gathered Borders

1. Pin the 43½" strips to either side of the center panel, with the gathers against the right side of the gray fabric. Stitch using a ½" seam allowance. Press the seam allowances toward the gray fabric. ❸

2. Repeat with the 39" strips at the top and bottom; press. ❹

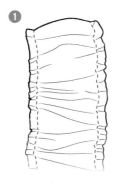

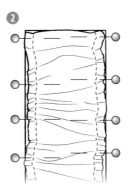

Attaching the Outer Borders

1. Trim two of the gray 3" outer-border strips to 43" for the top and bottom borders; set aside.

2. Trim two of the gray 3" outer-border strips to 46½". Pin the strips to the right and left sides of the quilt top; stitch using a ½" seam allowance. Press the seam allowances toward the gray fabric. ⑤

3. Repeat with the 43" strips at the top and bottom; press. ⑥

Finishing the Quilt

1. Cut the backing fabric into two lengths and join the pieces using a ¼" seam allowance. Press the seam allowances open. Trim the backing to equal the measurements of the quilt top, plus 4" on each edge.

2. Layer the quilt top with batting and backing (with the seam running horizontally); baste. Hand or machine quilt as desired. My quilt was stitched in a circular pattern over the doilies, and then in a swirling pattern within the rest of the center and the outer borders. The gathered borders were not quilted.

3. To bind the edges, use the gray 2½" strips and see "Binding" (page 89).

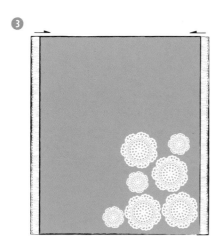

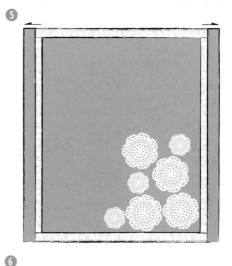

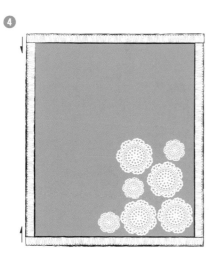

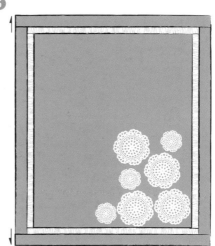

Square-within-a-Square PILLOW

Finished size: 18" x 18"

I love pillows. They make any house feel cozy and inviting. Here's a simple modern pillow based on a traditional design, with soft gathers in the center square for a touch of texture.

Materials

Yardage is based on 42"-wide fabric.

½ yard of light blue cotton fabric for center panel, accent border, and pillow back

½ yard of dark blue fabric for borders and pillow back

Cluster Stuff or fiberfill, 16-ounce bag

Cutting

From the light blue fabric, cut:
1 strip, 7½" x 14"
1 square, 7½" x 7½"
2 strips, 1" x 10½"
2 strips, 1" x 11½"

From the dark blue fabric, cut:
2 strips, 2" x 7½"
2 strips, 2" x 10½"
2 strips, 4" x 11½"
2 strips, 4" x 18½"

Assembling the Pillow

Use ¼" seam allowances unless otherwise indicated.

1. Set your sewing machine to the longest (basting) stitch. Gather the long edges of the 7½" x 14" light blue strip using a ⅛" seam allowance, holding the top thread by your thumb and index finger, near the spool, to put tension on the thread; see "Machine Ruffles and Gathers" (page 91).

2. Layer the gathered strip, right side up, on the light blue 7½" square. Loosen or tighten the gathers to make the strip fit the square. Baste around the perimeter.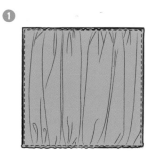

3. With right sides together and the gathers running vertically, pin the dark blue 2" x 7½" strips to the right and left sides of the square. Stitch. Press the seam allowances toward the dark blue fabric. ❷

4. Add the dark blue 2" x 10½" strips to the top and bottom of the unit. Press. ❸

5. Add the light blue 1" x 10½" strips to the right and left sides of the unit, and then the light blue 1" x 11½" strips to the top and bottom. Press. ❹

6. Finally, add the dark blue 4" x 11½" strips to the right and left sides of the unit, followed by the dark blue 4" x 18½" strips to the top and bottom. Press. ❺

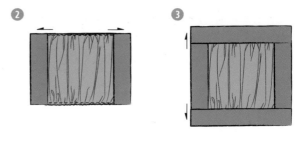

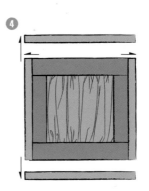

Piecing the Pillow Back

1. Cut the leftover light and dark blue fabrics of assorted widths into strips longer than 18½".

2. Sew the strips together to create a piece larger than 18½" square. Press the seam allowances in the same direction. Trim the piece to 18½" x 18½".

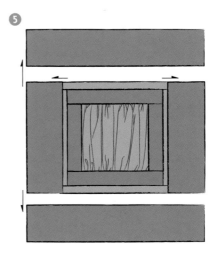

Finishing the Pillow

1. With right sides together, pin the pillow front and back pieces. Sew around the perimeter, leaving a 4" opening along a side parallel to the pillow-back seams. ❻

2. To avoid pointy corners on your pillow, see "Pillow Corners" (page 92).

3. Turn the pillow right side out, stuff, and hand stitch the opening closed using a ladder stitch (page 91).

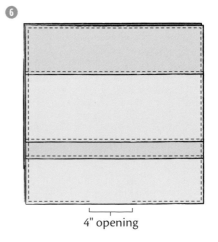

4" opening

All-Season SCARF

Finished size: Approximately 8" x 70"

Whether you want to dress up a simple outfit or need extra warmth, this scarf will become a go-to accessory. How many colors will you make it in?

Materials

Yardage is based on 60"-wide fabric.

1 yard of jersey (lightweight knit) fabric
Water-soluble marker
Elastic thread
Walking foot (optional, but very helpful)

Cutting

From the jersey fabric, cut:
2 strips, 8" x 60"
2 strips, 6" x 60"

Assembling the Scarf

Use ¼" seam allowances.

1. Pin and sew the 8" x 60" strips, right sides together, at the short ends. Press the seam allowances open. Repeat with the 6" x 60" strips.
2. Working on the right side of the 8"-wide pieced strip, mark a center line down the length of the strip using the water-soluble marker. Also mark a line 1¼" from each edge. ❶
3. To wind the elastic thread, see step 3 of the Cascading Spring Scarf (page 11).

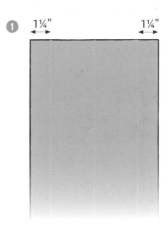

❶   1¼"   1¼"

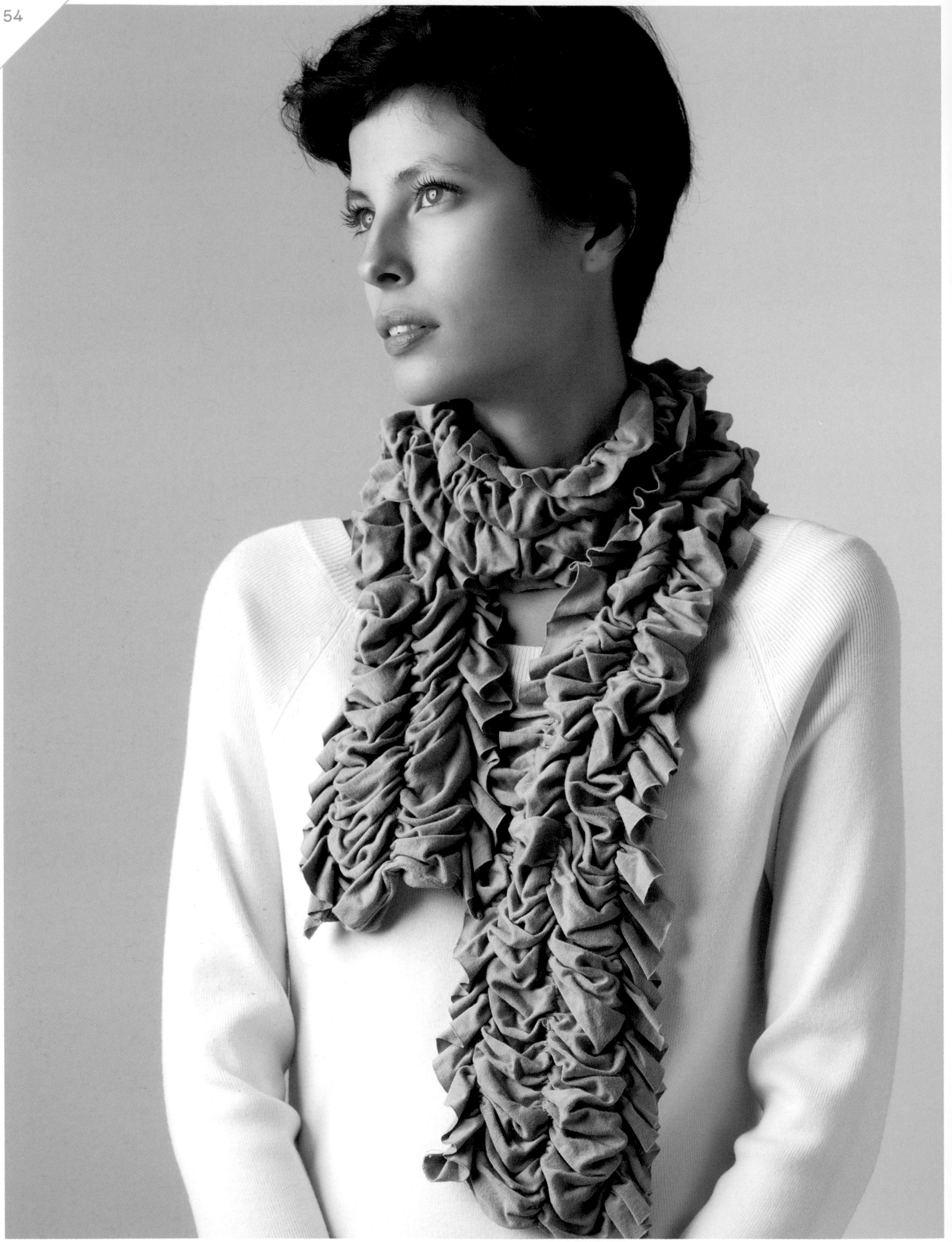

4. Set your sewing machine on the longest (basting) stitch and begin sewing on the center line. Hold the top thread between your thumb and forefinger, near the spool, to put tension on the thread; see "Machine Ruffles and Gathers" (page 91). Gather the entire length of the strip. Gather each edge on the marked line. ❷

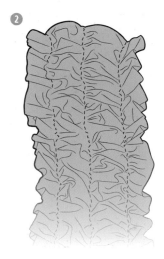

5. Trim the 6"-wide strip to match the length of the gathered strip. (The length will vary, depending on how your machine gathered the fabric.) Right sides together, pin the strips at the short ends, centering the 6"-wide strip. Switch to regular thread in the bobbin and stitch each end. Press the seam allowances open. ❸

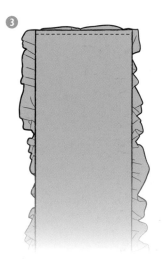

6. Cut any stray threads and turn the scarf right side out to make a large loop of fabric with the long edges open.

7. With the gathered strip on top, smooth the layers so the strips match in length. You may need to push and pull a little on the gathered strip.

8. Attach a walking foot, if you have one. Set the sewing machine to a regular stitch length and switch to regular thread in the bobbin.

9. Pin the length of the strips along one edge, erring on the side of more pins rather than fewer. Stitch on top of the gathers, making sure you're sewing through both layers. Repeat on the opposite edge and in the center. ❹

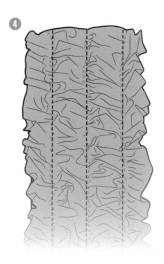

Decorative Bed PILLOW

Finished size: 14" x 15½"

Introduce texture to any bedroom with this lovely romantic pillow. My daughter has a pillow just like this one, and it adds a frilly visual punch to her bedding.

Materials

Yardage is based on 42"-wide fabric.

1 yard of white cotton fabric for pillow front and back

¼ yard of pale blue cotton fabric for flowers

Cluster Stuff or fiberfill, 16-ounce bag

Hot-glue gun and glue sticks (optional)

Cutting

From the white fabric, cut:

1 rectangle, 15" x 36"

2 rectangles, 15" x 16"

From the pale blue fabric, cut:

1 strip, 1½" x 42"

1 strip, 2" x 42"

1 strip, 2½" x 42"

Making the Gathered Pillow

Use ¼" seam allowances unless otherwise indicated.

1. To gather the white 15" x 36" rectangle, set the sewing machine on the longest (basting) stitch, pulling at least 3" of thread at the beginning to use in step 4.

2. Stitch along one long edge of the rectangle, again pulling at least 3" of thread at the end. Repeat on the opposite edge.

3. Gently pull a top thread on each edge to gather the piece until it measures approximately 10".

4. At each end of each gathered edge, carefully release 3" of fabric so it lies flat. ①

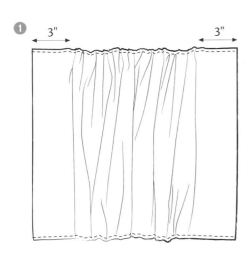

5. Layer the gathered piece on a white 15" x 16" rectangle, adjusting the gathers as necessary to make the gathered piece fit the plain piece. Pin. **2**

6. Baste around the perimeter of the layered pieces, stitching directly on top of the gathering stitches.

7. With right sides together, pin the layered pieces and the remaining white 15" x 16" rectangle. Using the first ¼" seam allowance as a guide, stitch the gathered edges of the pillow with a ½" seam allowance. On the remaining sides, stitch on top of your basting, leaving a 4" opening on one side for turning. **3**

8. To avoid "pointy" corners on your pillow, see "Pillow Corners" (page 92).

9. Turn the pillow right side out, stuff, and hand stitch the opening closed using a ladder stitch (page 91).

Adding the Flowers

These flowers have raw edges, and with time they will fray somewhat, depending on the fabric you use. If you prefer a finished look, zigzag or serge the raw edges before assembling each flower.

1. With a needle and thread, make a running stitch approximately ¼" from one long edge of each blue strip. Gently pull the thread to gather the strip, allowing it to curl over on itself to make two or three layers of "petals." **4**

2. Secure the gathers with a few tiny, tight stitches; then stitch through all layers at the base of each flower.

3. Hand stitch the flowers to the pillow front near one corner. Add a dab of hot glue to the backs of the flowers, if desired, pressing firmly until the glue is set.

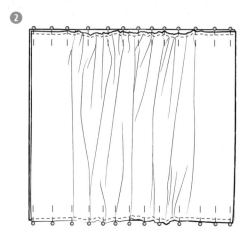

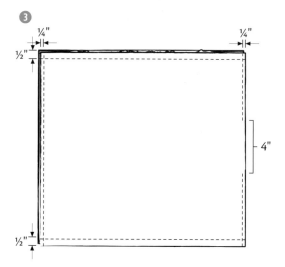

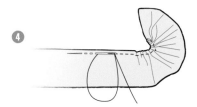

Market/Beach TOTE

Finished size: 17½" x 17½", excluding straps

I grew up in Southern California, and one of my favorite places besides the beach was the weekend farmer's market. This tote was inspired by those fun memories. I can just imagine the smell of the ocean and the beautiful colors of the locally grown produce that went into my tote.

Materials

Yardage is based on 42"-wide fabric.

1⅝ yards of cotton print fabric for gathered panel, lining, and handles

⅝ yard of Moda Cross Weave solid or mediumweight chambray* for tote exterior

1⅛ yards of lightweight fusible interfacing

See page 90.

Cutting

From the print fabric, cut:
2 strips, 12½" x 42"
1 rectangle, 18" x 36"
1 strip, 8" x 42"; cut in half to make 2 pieces, 8" x 21"

From the solid fabric, cut:
1 rectangle, 18" x 36"

From the fusible interfacing, cut:
1 rectangle, 18" x 36"

Making the Gathered Panels

Use ¼" seam allowances unless otherwise indicated.

1. Fold a print 12½" x 42" strip in half lengthwise, wrong sides together, so it measures 6¼" x 42". Sew along the long raw edges. Repeat with the remaining print 12½" x 42" strip.
2. With the seam centered on the back, press each strip flat, letting the seam allowances go in either direction. (Here they are shown up.) ❶

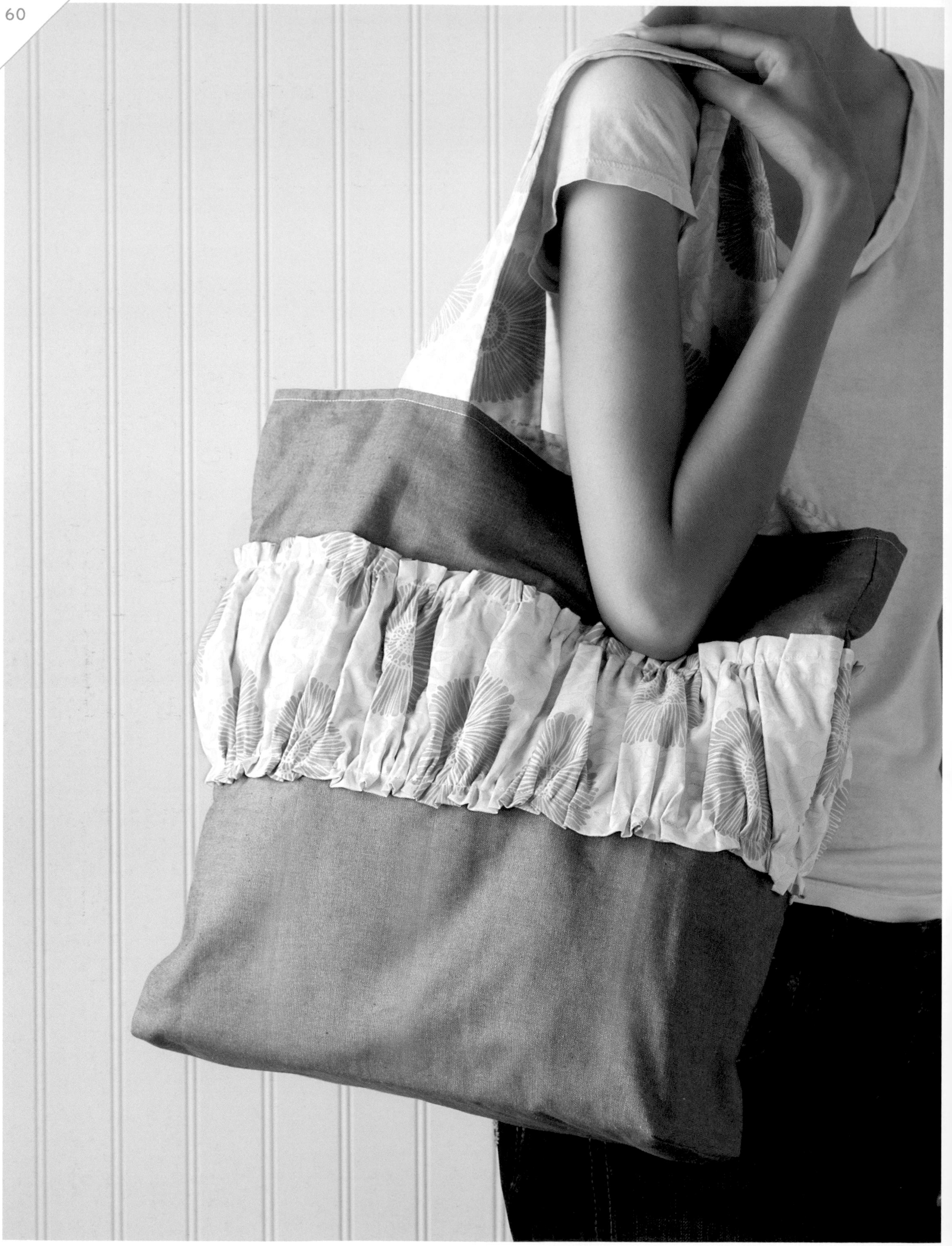

3. Set your sewing machine on the longest (basting) stitch. Hold the top thread between your thumb and forefinger, near the spool, to put tension on the thread; see "Machine Ruffles and Gathers" (page 91). Pull approximately 3" of thread at the beginning to release some gathers later, if necessary. Baste 1" from each folded edge of the strip to gather it, again pulling 3" of thread at the end. Repeat on the second strip.

4. Working on the right side of the solid 18" x 36" rectangle, pin a gathered strip 4" from each short edge. Set your sewing machine on a regular stitch and sew each strip to the rectangle ½" from the gathered edges. Remove the basting thread from each strip.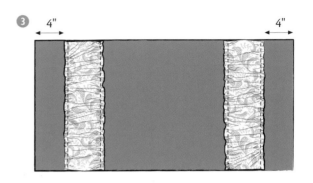

Making and Attaching the Straps

1. Fold, press, and topstitch the print 8" x 21" strips; see "Straps" (page 93).

2. Align the ends of one strap with an upper edge of the bag piece, placing the outer edges 5" from the sides as shown; pin. Machine baste the strap ends to the bag. Repeat at the opposite edge of the bag using the remaining strap.

Assembling the Bag

1. Fuse the interfacing to the wrong side of the print 18" x 36" rectangle.

2. With right sides together, pin the print rectangle to the bag exterior, sandwiching the straps in between. Sew the short ends of the rectangles to create a large loop of fabric. Press the seam allowances open.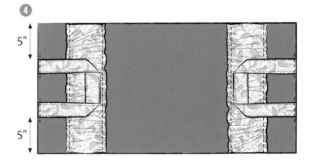

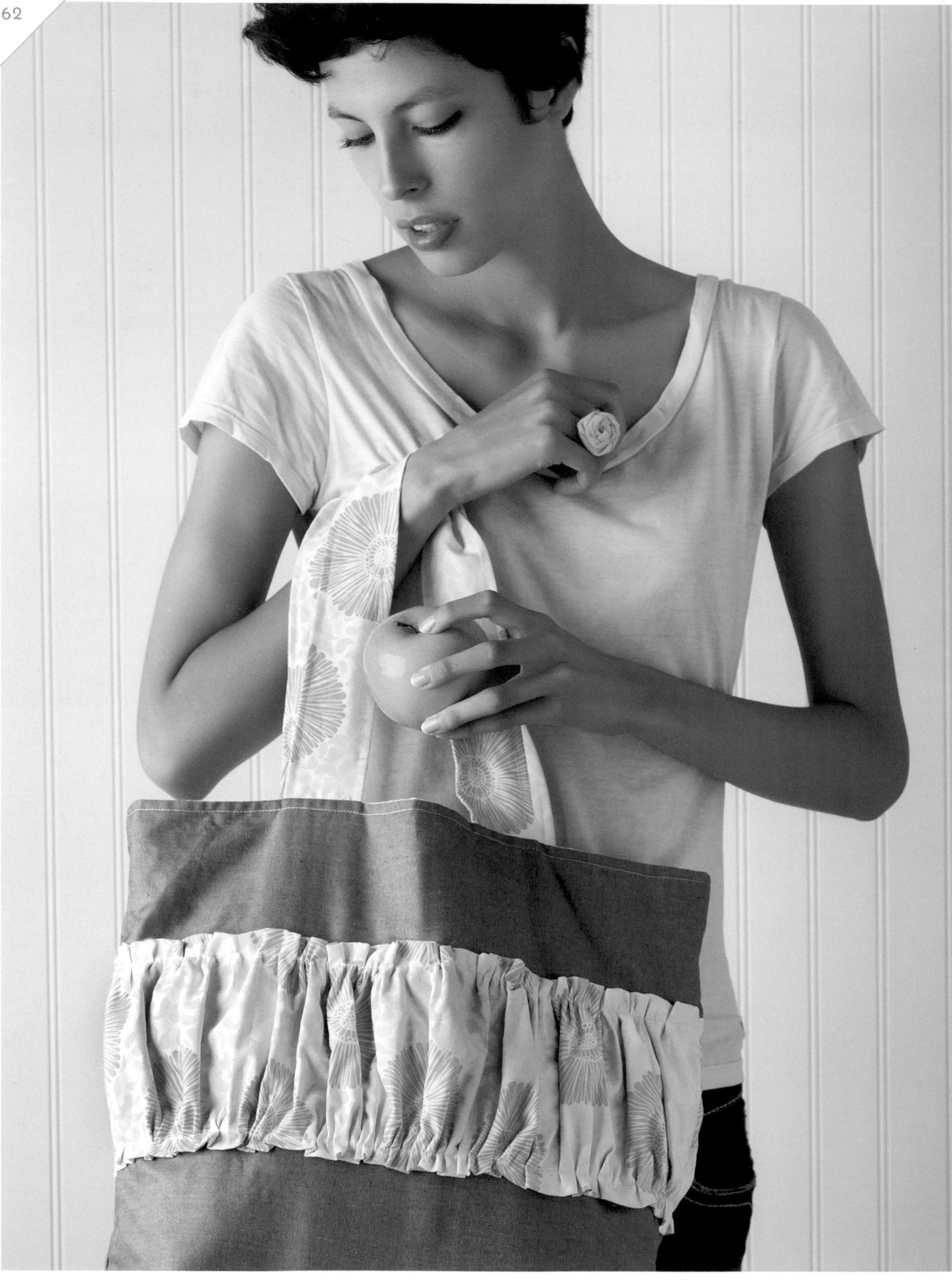

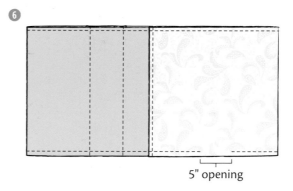

5" opening

3. With right sides still together, reposition the loop so the seams and the gathered strips match (at each end, a fold will form). Pin the long open edges on both sides. Stitch, leaving a 5" opening on one side of the lining for turning. ❻

4. To box the corners, position the bag sideways so one side seam of the lining is centered at the bottom, forming a point. (The seam allowances can go in either direction.) Measure and mark a stitching line perpendicular to the seam and 2" from the point. Sew on the marked line, backstitching at each end to secure. Leaving a ¼" seam allowance, trim the point to reduce the bulk. Repeat on the opposite corner of the lining and the remaining corners of the bag. ❼

5. Turn the bag right side out through the opening. Hand stitch the opening closed using a ladder stitch (page 91).

6. Tuck the lining inside the bag and topstitch the bag ¼" from the upper edge.

7. Optional: For a sturdier bottom, cut a piece of cardboard 4" x 14" and cover with a 5" x 15" or slightly larger piece of leftover print fabric. Glue the edges of the fabric to the back of the cardboard and let dry. Insert the piece into the bottom of the bag.

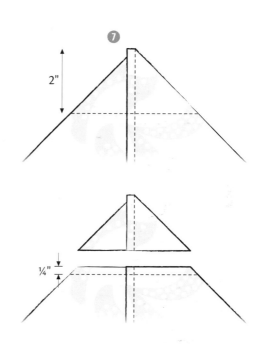

2"

¼"

Pleats

Chic Modern PILLOW

Finished size: 14½" x 15½"

Pillows are a must throughout my house, as decorating accents or just for relaxing. The cool, clean lines of this pleated pillow will surely make it the perfect addition to your home.

Materials

Yardage is based on 42"-wide fabric.

½ yard of yellowish-green solid
½ yard of muslin
Cluster Stuff or fiberfill, 16-ounce bag

Cutting

From the yellowish-green fabric, cut:
1 piece, 15" x 23"
1 piece, 15" x 16"

From the muslin, cut:
1 piece, 15" x 16"

Assembling the Pillow

Use ¼" seam allowances.

1. With the 15" x 23" rectangle running lengthwise, wrong side up, mark the sides as shown, starting 1½" from the top. Alternate 1" and 2" marks, ending with a mark 2½" from the lower edge. ❶
2. Starting at the lower edge, pinch the fabric at the first set of marks, making a crease. ❷

❶

❷

3. Bring the crease up to the second set of marks and pin on both edges, forming the first pleat. ❸

4. Move to the next set of marks and repeat the process. Continue to pinch, fold up, and pin the pleats all the way up the rectangle.

5. Press the pleats to set them. Once the pleats are set, unpin them.

6. Fold the first pressed pleat away from the rectangle and stitch ¼" from the creased edge. Repeat for all the pleats. ❹

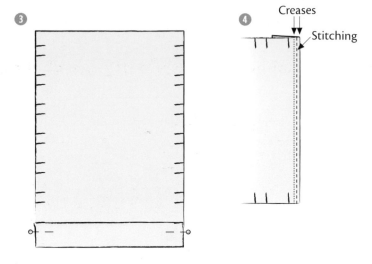

Tip: The stitched pleats will be on the *inside* of the finished pillow so you won't see them. On the front, you'll see only soft, elegant folds.

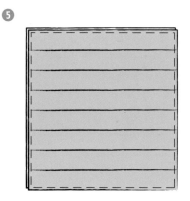

7. Layer the piece, *stitched side down and soft folds up*, on the 15" x 16" muslin piece, pinning through each pleat. Baste around the perimeter of the layered pieces. ❺

8. Right sides together, pin the soft-fold pillow front to the yellowish green 15" x 16" piece. Sew around the perimeter, stitching directly on top on your previous ¼" stitching and leaving a 4" opening on one unpleated edge for turning. ❻

9. Turn the pillow right side out, stuff, and hand stitch the opening closed using a ladder stitch (page 91).

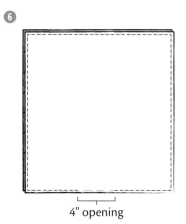

4" opening

The Favorite BAG

Finished size: 16½" x 11½", excluding strap

This stylish bag is perfect for weekdays or the weekend, and is practical in size and design. It's ideal for taking anywhere, which is why it's one of my favorite bags.

Materials

Yardage is based on 42"-wide fabric.

⅝ yard of large-scale print* for bag exterior
½ yard of coordinating fabric for lining
¼ yard of light aqua solid for flower
¾ yard of lightweight fusible interfacing
CD for corner template

See "Directional Patterns" (page 90).

Cutting

From the large-scale print, cut:
2 rectangles, 17" x 12"
1 strip, 6" x 24"

From the black-and-white print, cut:
2 rectangles, 14" x 12"
2 rectangles, 11" x 7"

From the fusible interfacing, cut:
2 rectangles, 14" x 12"

Making the Bag and Lining

Use ¼" seam allowances.

1. Use the CD to mark rounded corners at the bottom of the two large-scale exterior pieces. Trim on the marked lines. Set aside.
2. Fuse the interfacing to the wrong sides of the 14" x 12" lining pieces. Use the CD to mark and trim rounded corners as you did on the exterior rectangles.

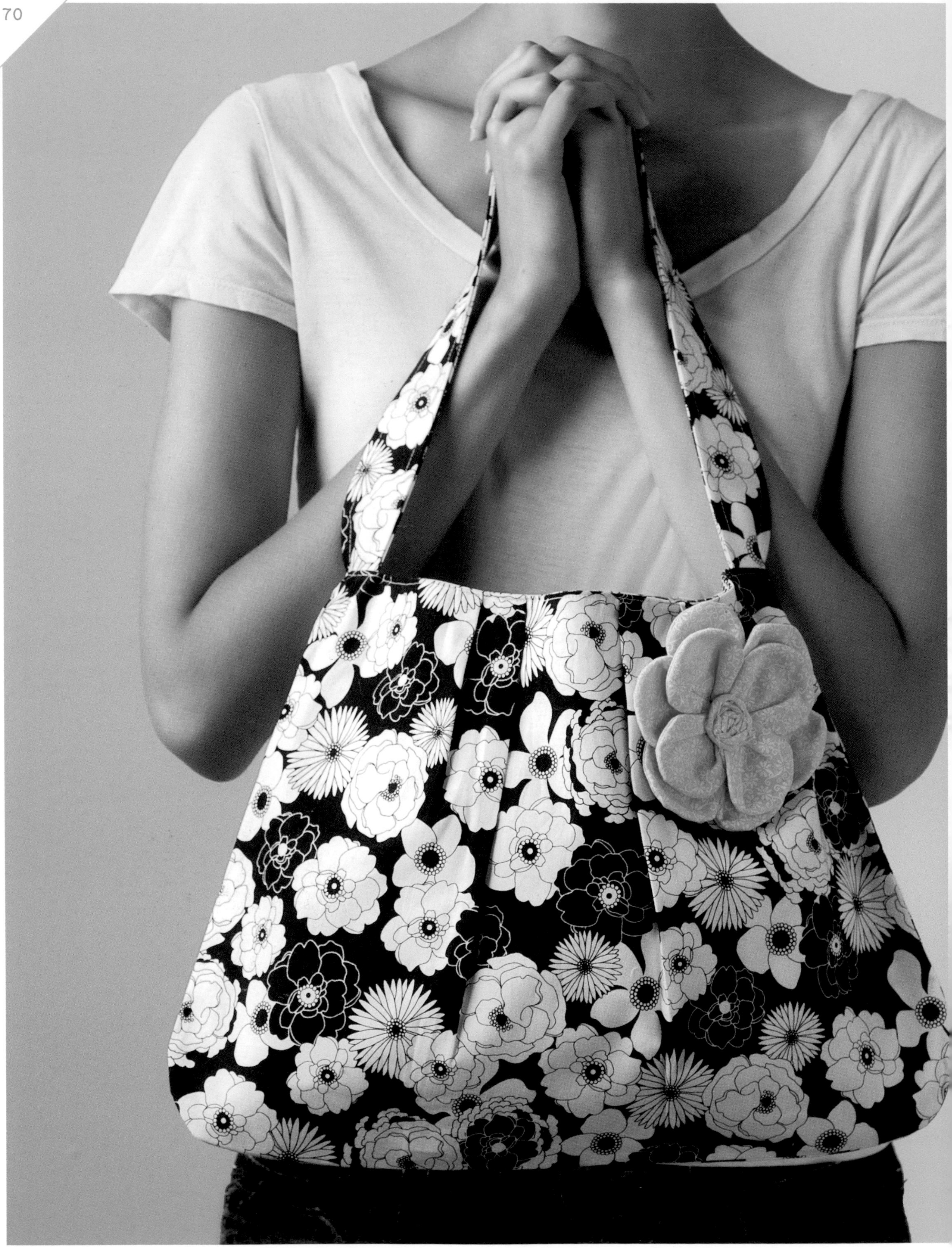

3. To angle the sides of the bag, lay your ruler on the wrong side of one exterior piece and draw a line from the beginning of the bottom curve to 1" from the side at the top, as shown. Trim on the line. Repeat on the opposite edge and the remaining exterior piece. Do the same on the lining pieces. ❷

4. To make the inside pocket, pin the two 11" x 7" lining rectangles right sides together. Sew around the perimeter, leaving a 3" opening on one long edge for turning. ❸

5. Clip the corners, turn right side out, and press. Topstitch the pocket using a ⅛" seam allowance, stitching the opening closed.

6. Center the pocket horizontally on the right side of one lining piece, 3" from the upper edge. Stitch around the sides and the bottom using a ¼" seam allowance, backstitching at the beginning and end. Divide the pocket as desired by stitching it vertically. ❹

7. Pin the lining pieces right sides together. Sew around the sides and bottom, leaving a 5" opening on one side for turning. Press the seams flat. Turn the lining right side out. ❺

8. Right sides together, pin and sew the bag exterior large-scale pieces. Press the seams flat and turn right side out. Measure and pin the midpoint of the upper edge on one side of the bag. ❻

❷ 1" 1"

3" opening

❺ 5" opening

Midpoint

9. Pleat the top edge as shown, folding the pleats inward and using the pin as a guide, until the edge measures 11½" from seam to seam. Pin the pleats. Repeat on the remaining bag exterior piece. **7**

10. Baste the top edge of the bag to secure the pleats. Turn the bag wrong side out and set aside.

Making the Strap

1. Fold, press, and topstitch the 6" x 24" strip; see "Straps" (page 93).

2. With the lining still right side out, center each strap end on each side seam, making sure not to twist the strap. Pin. Baste the strap ends ⅛" from the raw edges. **8**

Assembling the Bag

1. Insert the lining into the bag, right sides together, aligning the side seams and sandwiching the strap between the exterior and the lining. Pin the top edges; sew. **9**

2. Turn the bag right side out through the opening in the lining. Hand stitch the opening closed using a ladder stitch (page 91).

3. Tuck the lining into the bag. Edgestitch the bag ⅛" from the top edge.

4. To add the flower shown, see the Folded-Petal Flower (page 73).

11½"

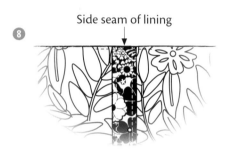

Side seam of lining

THE FAVORITE BAG

Folded-Petal FLOWER

Finished size: Approximately 4½" in diameter

This flower would look great on a purse, a pillow, or a sun hat, or you could even adorn your camera strap. Wherever you pin it, it's sure to be a lovely addition.

Materials

Yardage is based on 42"-wide fabric.

¼ yard of cotton print fabric
Pencil
Hot-glue gun and glue sticks
Felt circle, approximately 2½" in diameter
Pin back

Making the Petals

Use ¼" seam allowances unless otherwise indicated. For the petals, use the template (page 75).

1. Fold the fabric in half, right sides together with the selvages aligned.
2. Using the template, mark 10 petals along the raw edges of the fabric, leaving ½" between petals. ❶
3. With the fabric still folded, pin and sew on the marked lines. Cut out the petals, leaving a scant ⅛" seam allowance. ❷

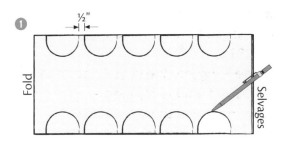

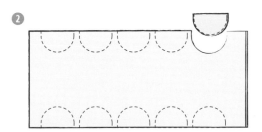

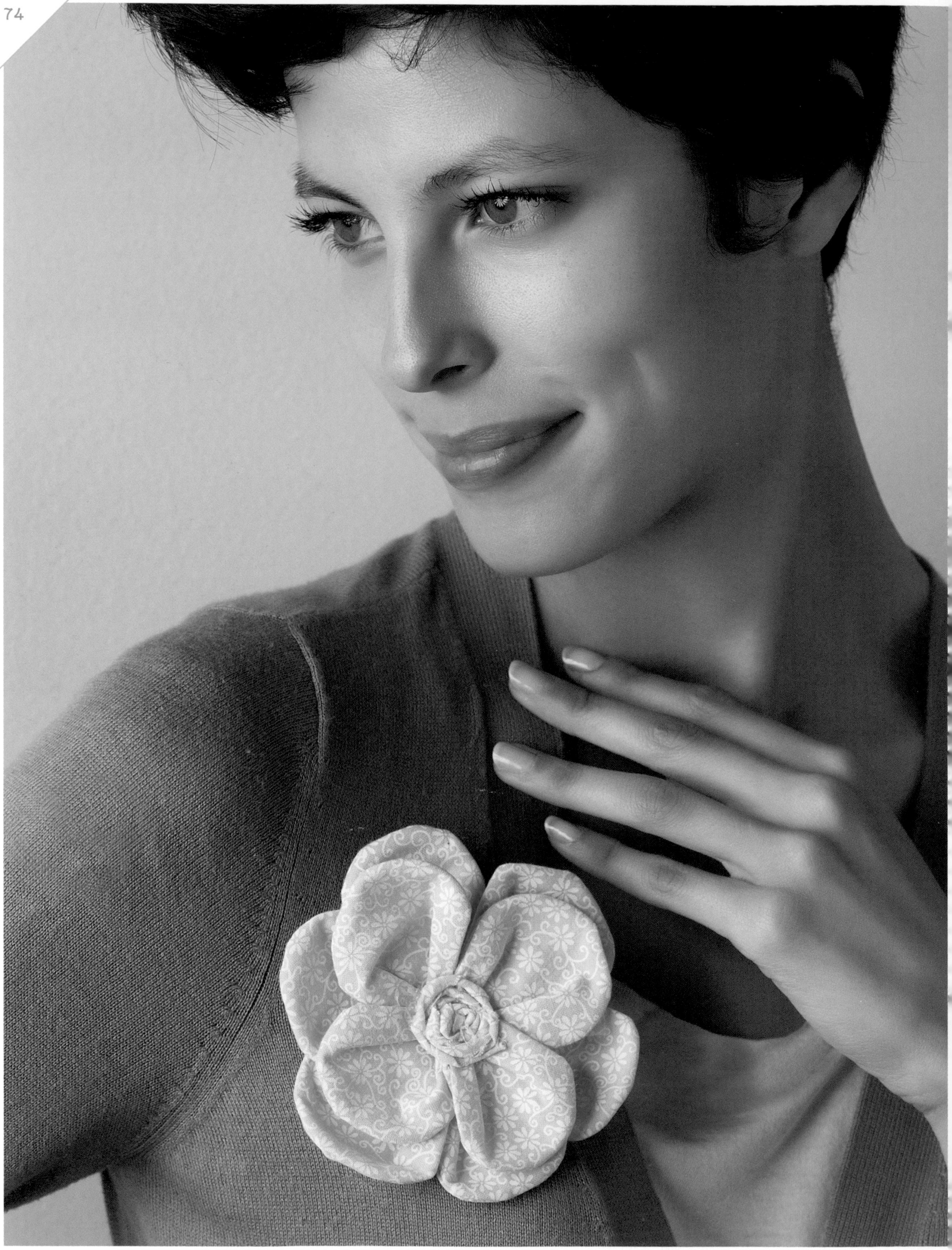

4. Turn the petals right side out and press. Mark the center of a petal along the raw edges with a pin. Make a pleat on each side, bringing the folds inward to meet at the center. Pin the pleats. Repeat for all the petals.

5. Stitch the pleated edges of each petal, removing the pins as you go. To save time and thread, chain stitch the petals (page 90). When finished, cut the petals apart.

Attaching the Petals

1. Dab a bit of hot glue onto the back of a petal at its base. Attach the petal with its raw edges at the center of the felt circle. Glue the next petal opposite the first, with the raw edges touching.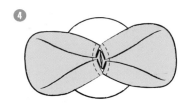

2. Glue the next two petals between the first two, overlapping the edges.

3. Repeat with two more petals on the opposite side of the circle to complete the bottom layer of petals.

4. Add the four remaining petals to make the top layer, spacing them between the bottom petals. If you want a fuller flower, make and attach even more petals.

Making the Flower Center

1. Cut a 1" x 10" strip from your leftover flower fabric.

2. To make the flower center, see steps 1–6 of "Making the Flower Ring" (page 31).

3. Dab a bit of hot glue on the back of the flower center and adhere it to the middle of the petals, pressing firmly until the glue is set.

4. Glue the flower to the pin back.

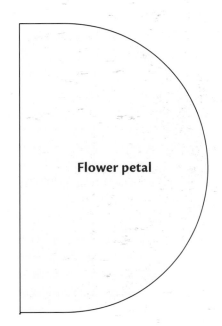

Flower petal

Everyday QUILT

Finished size: 39½" x 46½", excluding the pleated edging

This simple two-toned quilt, with its crisp pleated edging, will be a stylish addition to any nursery. Add a monogram to make it personal.

Materials

Yardage is based on 42"-wide fabric.

2⅜ yards of taupe solid for borders, backing, and pleated edging

1¾ yards of mediumweight cream fabric, prestitched in a crisscross or other design, for quilt center and borders

40" x 47" piece of batting

Cutting

From the cream fabric, cut:
1 rectangle, 29" x 36"
2 strips, 1½" x 39"
2 strips, 1½" x 34"
5 strips, 3" x 42"

From the taupe solid, cut:
2 strips, 2" x 36"
2 strips, 2" x 32"
2 strips, 1" x 41"
2 strips, 1" x 35"
9 strips, 2" x 42"
1 piece, 40" x 47"

Making the Quilt Top

Use ¼" seam allowances unless otherwise indicated.

1. With right sides together, pin the taupe 2" x 36" strips to the right and left edges of the cream 29" x 36" rectangle. Stitch. Press the seam allowances toward the darker fabric. Repeat with the taupe 2" x 32" strips at the top and bottom edges.

2. Add the cream 1½" x 39" strips to the right and left edges of the quilt top, followed by the cream 1½" x 34" strips at the top and bottom.

3. Add the taupe 1" x 41" strips to the right and left edges of the quilt top, followed by the taupe 1" x 35" strips at the top and bottom.

4. With right sides together, stitch the five cream 3" x 42" strips end to end to make one long strip. From this long strip, measure and cut two strips for side borders; sew them to the quilt top. Repeat to measure and cut top and bottom borders; sew them to the quilt top. ❶

> **Tip:** Measure and cut each side border so the seam is at least several inches from one end.

Adding the Pleated Edging

1. With right sides together, stitch the nine taupe 2" x 42" strips end to end to make one long strip. Press the seam allowances open.

2. At one end of the strip, fold ¼" to the wrong side; press. Fold the strip lengthwise, wrong sides together, and press the length of the strip, rolling it up as you go to make it easier to handle. ❷

3. Align the raw edges of the strip with the edge of the quilt top along one side. Leaving a 1" tail at the folded end of the strip, lower your sewing-machine needle into the strip. ❸

4. Take one stitch; then immediately pinch ¼" of fabric and fold it forward, under the needle, forming a small pleat. Sew over the first pleat just enough to secure it to the quilt top. ❹

5. Approximately 1" from the first pleat,

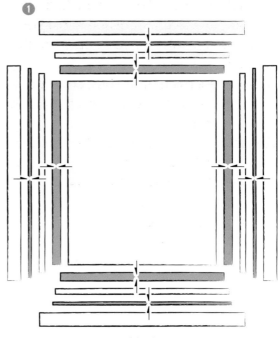

Assembly diagram

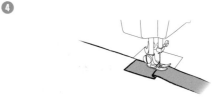

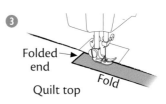

Folded end

Fold

Quilt top

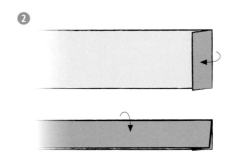

pinch another ¼" of the strip, fold it forward, and stitch. Continue folding and stitching pleats until you approach the first corner. ❺

6. Stop stitching ½" from the corner, backstitch, and take the quilt top from under the machine. ❻

7. Fold the next pleat at a 45° angle and stitch until the needle is ¼" from the raw edge of the adjacent side. ❼

8. Raise the needle, pivot the work, and immediately make another pleat. Continue to fold and stitch pleats until you reach the next corner; repeat the process at the remaining corners. ❽

9. Continue making pleats until you approach the point where you began. Make a pleat as close as possible to the folded end of the "tail." ❾

10. Measure and mark the strip 2½" beyond this last pleat. Take your work out from under the machine and cut the strip at the mark. ❿

Tip: This is definitely the time to "measure twice and cut once." If you cut the strip too short, you won't have enough fabric to make the final two pleats.

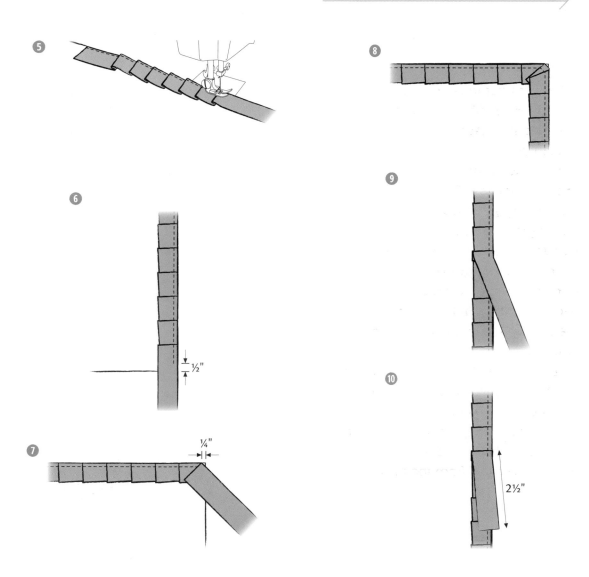

11. Slip the raw end approximately ¼" inside the folded end to make an arc of fabric. ⓫

12. Make the last two pleats, hiding the folded end under the final pleat. (You'll need to fiddle a bit with these pleats.) When you're satisfied with the pleats, stitch them to complete the edging. ⓬

13. Press the pleats for a crisp finish.

Assembling the Quilt

1. Layer the quilt top, batting, and backing in this order: the quilt top right side up, the backing right side down, and the batting on top. Pin the layers, making sure the edges of the batting, backing, and quilt top align precisely at the corners.

2. Stitch around the perimeter, angling the corners as you did when you attached the pleated edging. Leave an 8" opening along on one long edge for turning.

3. Carefully clip the corners to reduce the bulk. Turn the quilt right side out, folding the seam allowances of the opening to the inside. Hand stitch the opening closed using a ladder stitch (page 91).

4. Topstitch (page 93) the edges, stitching through all layers. ⓭

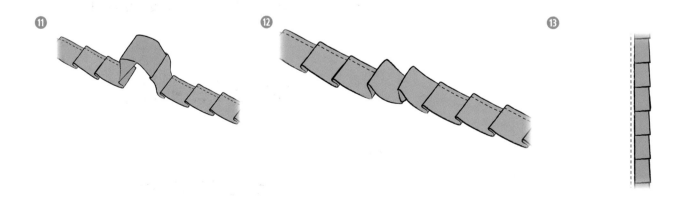

Schoolgirl SKIRT

Finished size: 4T to 5T

This little skirt can be for casual wear or for dress up. I call it the Schoolgirl Skirt because my daughter loves skirts, and I can see her wearing one each day of the school week.

Materials

Yardage is based on 42"-wide fabric.

⅝ yard of Moda Cross Weave solid or medium-weight chambray*

¾ yard of ½" elastic

See page 90.

Making the Skirt

Use ¼" seam allowances.

1. Measure around the little girl's waist; add half of that measurement for the cut width of the skirt. For example, my daughter's waist measurement was 22", so I added 11" to arrive at 33".
2. Measure from the girl's waist to where you want the skirt to end. I measured from my daughter's waist to her knees. Add 1¾" to that measurement for the cut length. Cut a piece of fabric to these measurements.
3. Fold the skirt right sides together at the shorter edges and stitch, creating a tube. Press the seam allowances open.
4. Decide which raw edge will be the top of the skirt. At that edge, fold ¼" to the wrong side and press. Fold another 1" to the wrong side and press. ❶

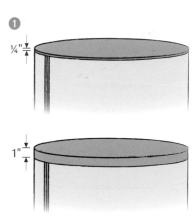

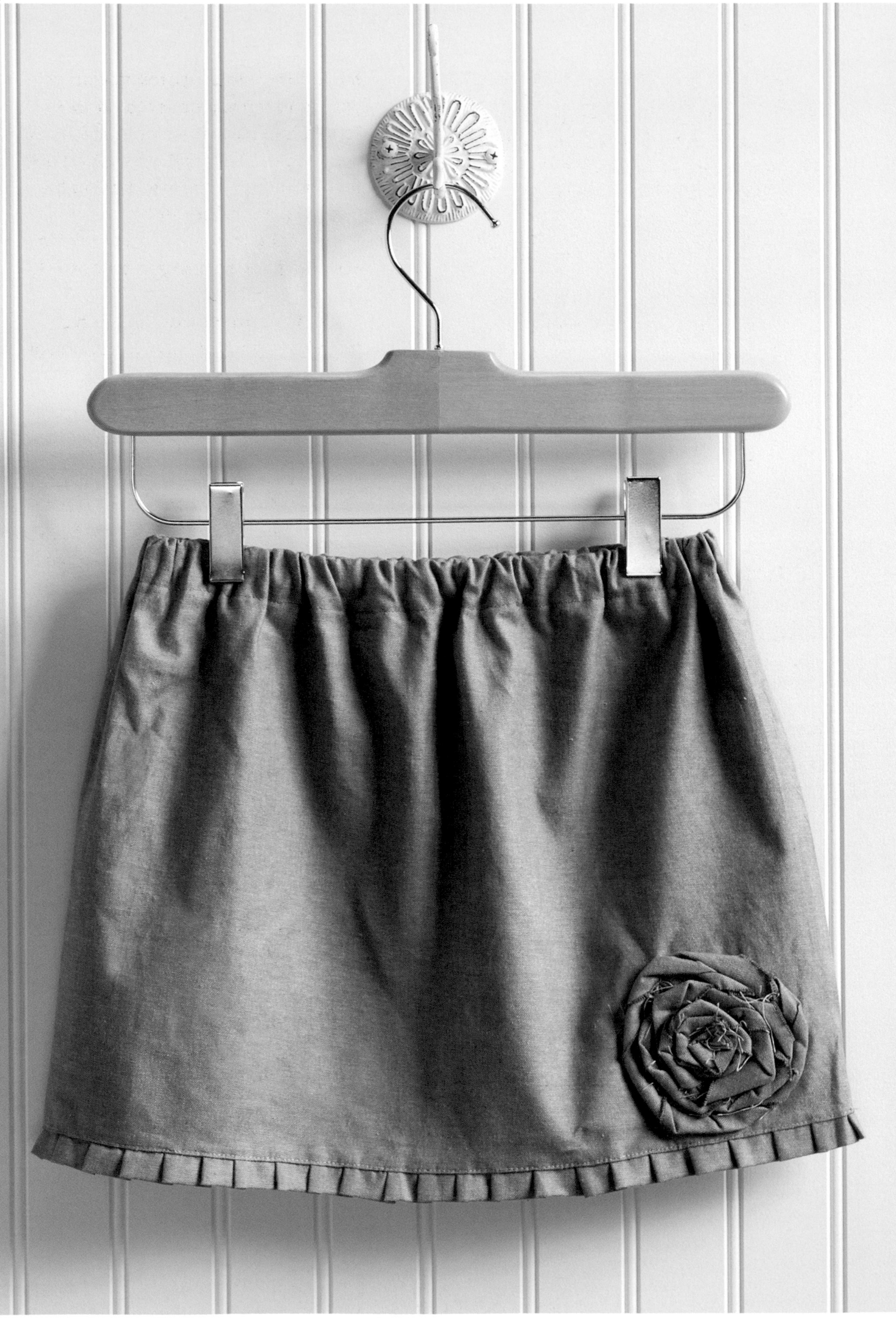

5. Stitch ¼" from the first fold to create a casing, leaving a 2" opening for inserting the elastic. ❷

6. Cut the elastic to the child's waist measurement to ensure a snug (but not too tight) fit. Attach a safety pin to one end of the elastic and feed it through the opening in the casing, going all the way around to the other side of the opening. Overlap the ends ½" and pin with the safety pin. Try the skirt on the child and shorten the elastic if needed. Stitch the ends securely by hand or machine.

7. Machine stitch the opening closed and turn the skirt right side out.

Making the Pleated Edge

1. From the leftover fabric, cut two strips, 1½" x 42". Sew the strips end to end to make one long strip. Press the seam allowances open.

2. At one end of the strip, fold ¼" to the wrong side; press. Fold the strip lengthwise, wrong sides together, and press the length of the strip, rolling it up as you go to make it easier to handle.

3. To fold and stitch the pleats, see steps 3–5 (pages 78 and 79), replacing "quilt top" with "skirt" and disregarding the reference to the corner.

4. To make the final pleats and tuck the end into the beginning, see steps 9–13 (pages 79 and 80).

5. Press the seam allowances toward the skirt. Edgestitch, sewing through all layers. ❸

Making the Flower

1. From the leftover fabric, cut two strips, 1½" x 42". Cut one strip in half; discard the other half. Sew the ends of the strips together to make one strip. Press the seam allowances open.

2. Fold the strip in half lengthwise, wrong sides together. Fold again to make the end ⅜" wide.

3. Mark where you want to begin the flower. I stitched mine on the lower-left front of the skirt, with its edges approximately 1½" from the side seam and ½" from the pleated edge.

4. Position the strip on the skirt and stitch across the end to secure it. To twist and stitch the strip, see steps 3–6 of Flower-Bouquet Pillow (page 30). (Note: You won't need to add another strip as shown on the pillow.)

❷
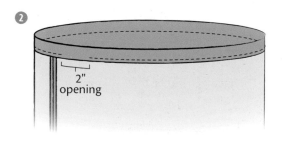
2" opening

❸
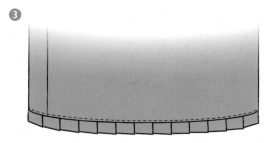

Handy TOTE

Finished size: 11½" x 14½"

My daughter and I both have a love of totes. This pleated bag can be used by Mom as a small tote for her sewing needs, or as a big tote for a little girl who has a lot to carry from one important date to another.

Materials

Yardage is based on 42"-wide fabric.

1 yard of coordinating fabric for lining and pocket
¾ yard of cotton print for tote exterior and straps*
½ yard of accent fabric for bow
1⅛ yards of medium-weight fusible interfacing
Water-soluble marker

See "Directional Patterns" (page 90).

Cutting

From the exterior fabric, cut:
2 rectangles, 12" x 21"
2 strips, 5" x 21"

From the lining fabric, cut:
1 rectangle, 12" x 29½"
1 rectangle, 7" x 12"

From the bow fabric, cut:
2 strips, 6" x 42"

From the interfacing, cut:
2 rectangles, 12" x 15"
1 rectangle, 7" x 12"

Assembling the Pleated Bag

Use ¼" seam allowances unless otherwise indicated.

1. With an exterior fabric 12" x 21" rectangle *wrong side up* and running lengthwise, mark the side edges as shown, starting 2" from the top. Alternate 1" and 2" marks, ending with marks 3" from the lower edge. Repeat on the remaining rectangle. ❶
2. Starting at the lower edge, pinch the fabric at the 3" marks, making a crease. To fold and pin the pleats, see steps 3–6 of the Chic Modern Pillow (page 68). Repeat with the remaining rectangle.

Tip: The stitched edges of the pleats will be on the *inside* of the finished tote so you won't see them. On the front, you'll see only soft, elegant folds.

3. Fuse an interfacing 12" x 15" rectangle to each bag piece *on the side with the stitched pleats.* Baste ⅛" around the perimeter of each piece.

4. With right sides together and the soft folds on the front pointing *down*, pin the bag pieces at the bottom edges. Stitch using a ¼" seam allowance; press the seam allowances open. Set the unit aside. ❷

Assembling the Lining

1. To make the pocket, fuse the interfacing 7" x 12" piece to the wrong side of the lining 7" x 12" piece. Fold the piece right sides together so it measures 7" x 6". Sew around the three raw edges, leaving a 3" opening on one side for turning. Clip the corners. ❸

2. Turn the pocket right side out through the opening and stitch closed using a ladder stitch (page 91).

3. Center the pocket approximately 3" from one short edge of the lining piece with the fold at the top. Edgestitch (page 93) the pocket, backstitching at the beginning and end. ❹

Assembling the Bag

1. To fold, press, and topstitch the 5" x 21" strips, see "Straps" (page 93).

2. Measure the total length of the bag exterior unit and trim the lining to that length. Align the ends of one strap with one of the short edges of the lining, placing the outer edges of the strap 3" from the sides of the lining as shown; pin. Baste the strap ends to the lining. Repeat at the opposite edge with the remaining strap. ❺

❷

❸

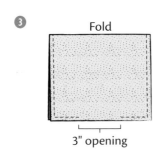

Fold

3" opening

❹

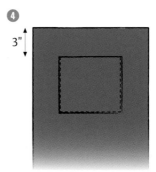

3"

❺

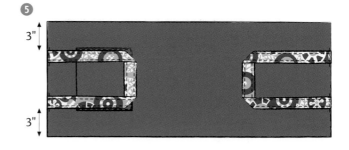

3"

3"

3. With right sides together and raw edges aligned, pin the bag exterior and lining (with the straps sandwiched in between) along the short edges. Stitch, creating a loop of fabric. Press the seam allowances open. **6**

4. Reposition the loop so the seams and the soft folds match. Pin the edges. Sew, leaving a 5" opening on one edge of the lining for turning. **7**

5. To box the corners, reposition the bag sideways so one side seam is centered at the bottom. (The seam allowances can go in either direction.) Measure and mark a stitching line perpendicular to the seam and 1½" from the point. Sew on the marked line, backstitching at the beginning and end to secure. Leaving a ¼" seam allowance, trim the corner point to reduce the bulk. Repeat on the remaining corners. **8**

6. Turn the bag right side out through the opening. Hand stitch the opening closed using a ladder stitch (page 91).

7. Tuck the lining inside the bag and topstitch the upper edge.

Making the Bow

1. Cut one strip in half to make two strips, 6" x 21"; set one piece aside for your scrap basket. Sew the 42" and 21" strips together end to end to make one long strip. Press the seam allowances open.

2. Fold the strip lengthwise, right sides together. Trim each end at a 45° angle as shown below. Stitch the long raw edges and the ends, leaving a 6" opening for turning. **9**

3. Turn the strip right side out. Hand stitch the opening closed using a ladder stitch (page 91).

4. Edgestitch (page 93) the three stitched edges. Tie the strip into a bow and pin it to the tote.

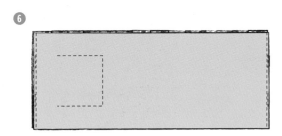

6

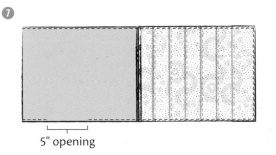

7

5" opening

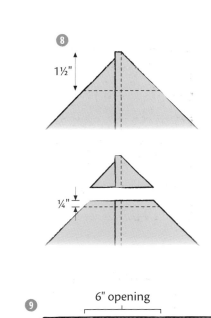

8

1½"

¼"

9

6" opening

Tips, Terms, and Techniques

If you're new to sewing, you'll need to know the terms and techniques used throughout the projects. Even if you've had lots of sewing experience, review this section to ensure that your project turns out as you planned. Following are the basics, organized alphabetically.

Appliqué Stitch

Use this versatile stitch to attach the doilies to the quilt in the Appliqué Doily Quilt (page 47).

1. Hold the doily (or other appliqué) firmly between your thumb and index finger. With a single length of knotted thread, bring the needle up through the quilt fabric from the wrong side, and then through the very edge of the doily.
2. Insert the needle straight down into the fabric, directly opposite the spot where the needle came up. To take the next stitch, bring the needle up through the fabric and into the edge of the doily, approximately ⅛" from the previous stitch. Continue stitching around the shape, finishing with a knot on the back of the fabric. ❶

Binding

A double-fold binding on a quilt provides a neat, durable edge. Following are the instructions for binding the Appliqué Doily Quilt (page 47).

1. With right sides together, join the 2½" gray strips on the diagonal to make one long strip. ❷
2. Press the seam allowances open. Press the strip in half lengthwise, wrong sides together.
3. Leaving an 8" to 10" tail at the beginning, sew the binding to the quilt top using a ¼" seam allowance. Miter the corners as shown. ❸

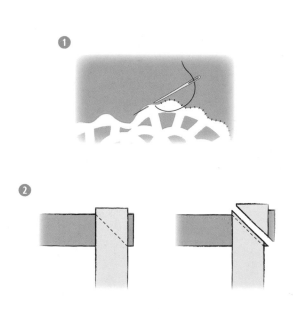

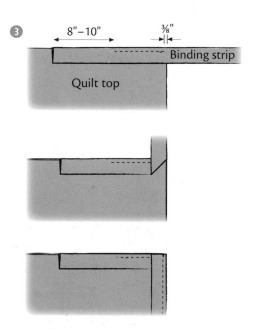

4. Stop sewing approximately 12" from the beginning and backstitch. Overlap the end of the strip with the beginning 2½" and trim. Sew the two ends together as shown and trim, leaving a ¼" seam allowance. Press the seam allowances open. Reposition the binding on the quilt and finish sewing. ❹

5. Fold the edge of the binding to the back and hand stitch it in place, mitering the corners. ❺

Chain Stitching

When you're stitching many of the same kind of units, like in the Folded-Petal Flower (page 73), it's most efficient to sew one right after the other without breaking the thread or taking your work from under the machine. Once finished, simply clip the thread between the units. ❻

Chambray

This light- to mediumweight smooth cotton fabric has colored warp (lengthwise) threads and white weft (crosswise) threads. Similar fabrics are sometimes referred to as "cross weave."

Directional Patterns

A printed fabric whose motifs run only one way, such as flowers on standing stems, has what's referred to as a directional pattern. You'll want to cut pieces for a project like the Handy Tote (page 85) lengthwise, orienting the pattern so it runs "up" on both sides of the finished tote. ❼

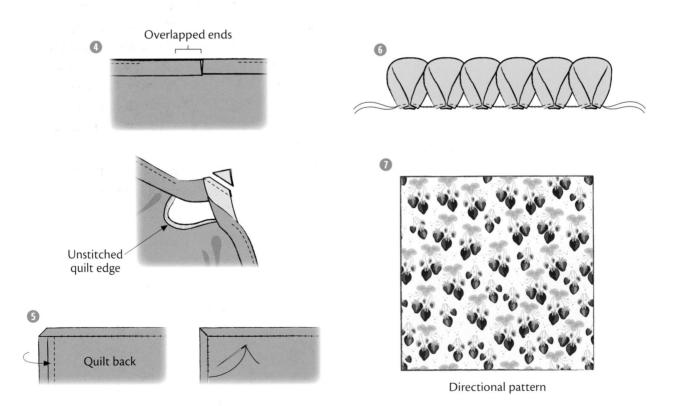

❹ Overlapped ends

Unstitched quilt edge

❺ Quilt back

❻

❼

Directional pattern

Hot-Glue Gun

This popular crafting tool has either a dual-temperature or single-temperature control. If you have a dual-temperature gun, set it on high to begin with; then turn it to low. Be aware that hot glue will melt Styrofoam, so use a glue gun with a low-temperature setting for projects like the Spring-Blossom Wreath (page 17) and Decorative Hanging Globes (page 15). When possible, put the glue on the fabric, not directly onto the Styrofoam. Other tips for using hot glue:

- Experiment with your glue gun to see how quickly the glue comes out before you begin a project.
- Use just a dab—not a glob—of glue.
- Rest the glue gun on a sturdy paper plate to catch any drips.
- Finally, to prevent burns, use great caution with your glue gun.

Ladder Stitch

This stitch is one of the most invisible hand-sewing stitches, making it the perfect choice for stitching the opening closed on a pillow or other project that's turned through an opening in a seam.

1. Using a single strand of thread knotted at the end, bring the needle up through either fold of the opening at the point where the machine stitching stops. Cross over to the opposite fold and take a stitch into the fold, "tunneling" forward approximately ⅛".

2. Cross back to the opposite fold and continue the stitching pattern until you reach the end of the opening. Your crossing stitches will resemble the rungs on a ladder. Every few stitches, gently pull the thread to close the opening. ⑧

3. At the end of the opening, take a few tiny stitches, knot the thread, and stitch down into the seam to "pop" and bury the knot.

Machine Ruffles and Gathers

In many of these projects, you'll gather a fabric strip or piece by machine. Hold the top thread, near the spool, between your thumb and forefinger to increase the tension on the thread. Stitch using the longest (basting) stitch on your machine. The fabric will begin to "ruffle" as you sew. It takes a bit of practice to find out how tightly you must hold the top thread, so be sure to experiment with your machine and a scrap of the fabric. ⑨

If you have a ruffling presser foot, by all means experiment with it, following the manufacturer's instructions.

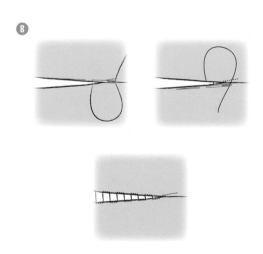

Pillow Corners

The corners of any square or rectangular pillow have a tendency to become "pointy" once the pillow is stuffed. To avoid that look, stitch the pillow pieces around the perimeter as instructed in the project, pivoting at the corners. Next, measure and mark 1" from each corner, along each line of stitching, and draw a diagonal line connecting the marks. Note that on projects with gathered pillow fronts, the seam allowances on adjacent sides will be different widths, but that doesn't change the technique; simply measure 1" from the stitched corner in each direction to mark and sew the diagonal line. **10**

Seam Allowance

Each project specifies a seam allowance, typically ¼". A seam allowance is the distance from the stitching, by hand or by machine, to the raw edge or edges of the fabric. The throat plate on most sewing machines has markings for various seam widths. A patchwork presser foot, when aligned with the raw edges, produces a ¼" seam allowance; check to see if the manufacturer of your machine offers a patchwork foot. When it comes to seam allowances, the most important tip is this: be consistent! Your project will go together more easily and look better when it's finished if you stitch with a consistent seam allowance. **11**

10

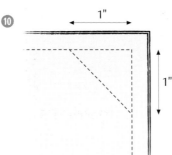

11

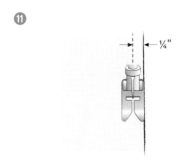

Seam Finishes

You have several choices when it comes to finishing seams.

1. After you press the seam allowances open, stitch each separately using a medium-length, medium-width zigzag stitch; trim close to the stitching, if necessary. Most of the projects call for pressing the seam allowances open.

2. You can also zigzag the seam allowances together, trimming close to the stitching. Press the seam allowances to one side. This technique is faster than zigzagging the seam allowances separately, but it does add bulk. ⑫

Straps

Several of the projects include straps. Fold the strip in half lengthwise, wrong sides together, and press a crease. Open the strip and turn the raw edges in to meet the pressed crease. Refold the strip, encasing the raw edges. Topstitch the edges (below). ⑬

Topstitching

Stitching close to the finished edge of any project gives it a neat, tailored look. Topstitching is usually done ¼" from the finished edge; edgestitching is even closer, typically ⅛". In either case, set your machine to a medium-length stitch. ⑭

Water-Soluble Marker

This marking pencil or pen makes marks that disappear with the application of a little water.

⑫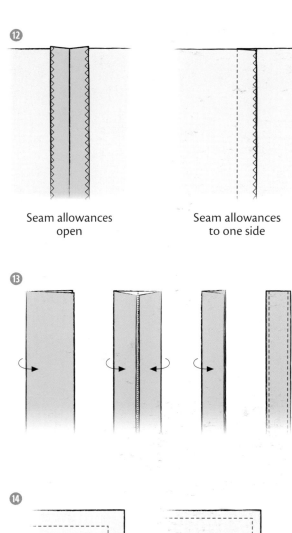

Seam allowances open

Seam allowances to one side

⑬

⑭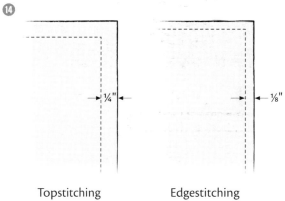

¼"

⅛"

Topstitching

Edgestitching

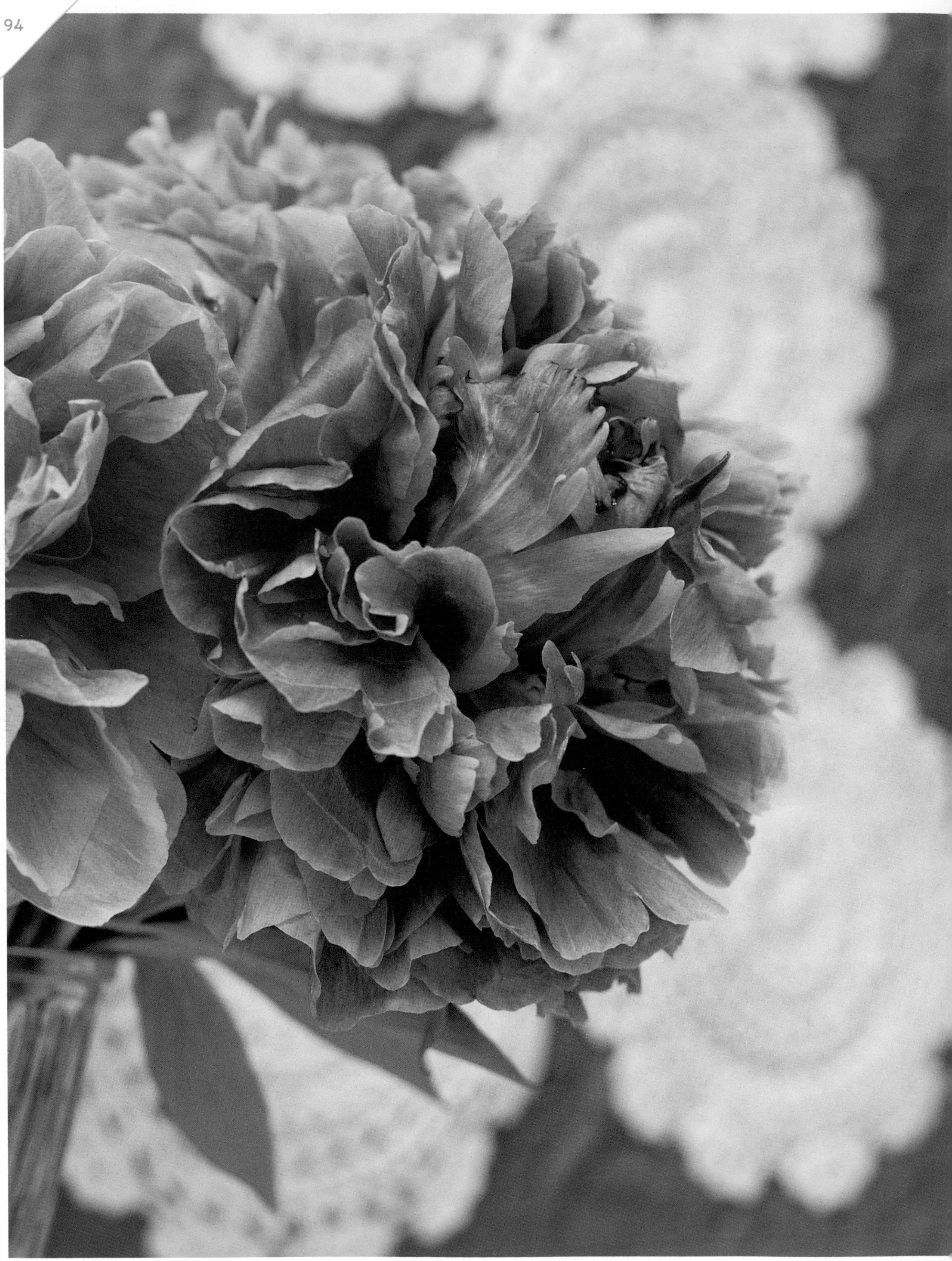

About the AUTHOR

Vanessa is wife to a great man and mother to three young boys and one little girl. They run her world, but when they're at work and school, she engages her creativity with fabric. For V and Co. Vanessa designs and sews an array of handbags, quilts, fabric jewelry, scarves, and accessories for the home.

She wasn't always a designer. Her first attempt at sewing in high school was frustrating, and she vowed never to try again. But she wanted to make things so badly that she gave it another try in her mid 20s, only to fail, try again, and fall in love.

When not sewing or blogging, Vanessa enjoys reading, thrifting, decorating, organizing everything in sight, and taking walks with her husband. Vanessa finds great happiness in her work, and she feels blessed to have frequent breaks from it to enjoy the most important thing in life: her family. She lives in Marion, Iowa.

There's More Online!

Visit Vanessa's site,
www.VanessaChristenson.com,
where she writes about her design
endeavors and her adventures as a mom.
Find more books on sewing and crafting at
www.martingale-pub.com.